My 100 Homies & Phonies of Hollywood

Sexy Courtney
Anytime Anyplace

A Story of an Ordinary Celebrity

By Pierre

Pierre

Published in the United States by Pierre & Pierre
An imprint of BBS Publishing group
A division of My House, Inc.

Library of Congress Cataloging-in-Publishing Data
"My 100 Homies and Phonies of Hollywood"/Pierre.
p. cm

ISBN 773-9311-867-5309

1. Pierre 2. Comedians-United States-Biography
2. African American Comedians-Biography. 4. Actors-United States-Biography 5. African American actors-Biography. I. Title
3.

PN2278.M6998A3 2010
797.7'6038902-dc32 2010905564
[B]

Printed in the United States on acid-free paper

www.thegreatestcomic.com
987665912
First edition
Book Designed by BJ Nartker

Table of Contents

Acknowledgements

I would like to thank GOD whom I recently met. I truly appreciate all that I've been through, because if just one thing were different I wouldn't be where I am. I thank my mom (R.I.P.) who always believed in me, even when it came to me dreaming of show business. Not once did she tell me not to pursue my dream. I thank my father for making me stubborn and showing me I can handle anything thrown at me. I want to thank my family and friends for believing in me *and* not believing in me. Both gave me the drive. Thank you to my homeboy, Joe P., who has been there through it all; we're like brothers. He is a true friend in all senses of the word. Thanks to all the managers and agents who put up with me, as I did with them. And to my special female friends who've supported me like you wouldn't believe. There is nothing better for a man than a woman who supports him unconditionally. I always finish what I start, out of respect for you listening to me for hours talking about my dreams. You don't understand what that meant to me.

Also thanks to the best undiscovered writing mind in the business: my editor, Akilah Webster. Girl, you the truth.

To all my show business competition: in the big picture, there's no competition. What's meant for you will be yours. What's not will never be. Jealousy doesn't belong in this business.

And last but not least, to my fans—you have no idea what receiving a compliment did for my self esteem at that moment, or how it helped push me through another day. I will always be indebted.

Foreword

Written by Paul Mooney

For starters a nigga named Pierre is already phony and I hope his book isn't as phony. This is an opportunist. I remember meeting this light-skinned nigga years ago. He thought he was White. He was trying to pass for White and I had to break that face and tell him what he was.

I mean if Pierre doesn't become famous it won't be because he didn't try, because he tried to steal fame. He did everything. He can actually sell a refrigerator to an Eskimo. He's about the slickest nigga I ever met. I hope his book does well because he deserves a best seller; he really does, because he's a bestseller. He sells himself to everyone. He plays this humble pie bullshit like he wouldn't hurt a fly. He actually reminds me of a White serial killer, he bears watching. But the good thing is he's got some talent, but he's got a lot of bullshit.

As Paul Mooney I'm happy for him and I'll be happy for you if you buy this book. Thank you.

My Introduction

One thing you'll learn about me is I keep it real; sometimes too real. Now I'm not writing this book out of revenge or dislike for anyone. This book came about one night when I was on stage in Atlanta just messing around, and someone yelled out "How was it working with Halle Berry?" I told them the story of our first meeting (you'll read about that) and had the crowd laughing. Then someone asked me about Tupac. This went on for 30 minutes. I had to cut my set short or I would have been there all night. Even as I went to my car, people were still asking me to tell them about other celebrities. On the drive home I thought about what had just occurred in the club, and the more I thought about it, the more I realized how often this happened to me. It seemed like everywhere I went, people were always asking about my experiences with other celebrities. At that moment, I knew it was time for me to write this book, before someone else does.

People sometimes have no idea how normal celebrities are behind closed doors. We're truly just like you, and many of us came from humble beginnings. No one in this book was born a celebrity but they all became one. I have a tremendous amount of respect for the people in these pages as artists. Now, as people…that's another story.

These are the stories I remember as I remember them. I was surprised that I could remember so much detail, but I guess when things affect you, you can always recall them. Now some of the people in these stories may not remember, because it probably didn't affect them. But I remember. They didn't think I would turn out to be anything. I have performed with many great and not so great artists, be it on stage, TV or in movies. Some were brief encounters, some were much longer. There's no need for me to lie, embellish or fabricate these stories. I'm not doing this for money and I fear no one.

I say some things in this book and sometimes speak in a manner that is reflective of me at the time of these incidents and encounters. That was then. I've come a long way. I wouldn't say, do or feel some of those things now.

So, this is my gift to the fans. Enjoy.

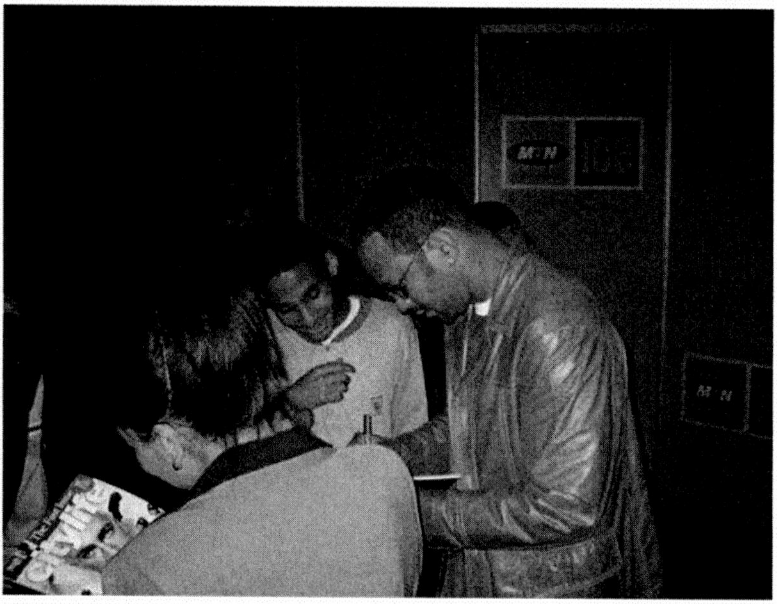

JONE (*jonin', to jone*) [verb] to verbally insult someone, to make fun of, to lower someone's self esteem, to degrade, also known in different parts of the country as playing the dozens, snappin', baggin', rankin', clownin', signifyin'

Pierre

My Mini Biography

Life throws you many curves, some good, some bad. It's how you handle those curves that will determine how smoothly your life turns out. I was never good at handling certain things, but great at handling other things. There is no gray area for me. I also love challenges. I'm fearless when it comes to trying new things. I don't believe the common path was made for me. If everyone is going right then I need to go left. Let me go through the door first. This thought process has been both rewarding and difficult at times.

Early on in life, I realized I was gifted with the ability to make people laugh. That's the one gift I'm so grateful to have. I don't think there's a greater gift, other than to have the ability to have total love in your heart. Making someone laugh is powerful. You can change a person's mood so quickly. People gravitate to funny people.

I was always amazed at how quick-witted my father was, and how his words would fit perfectly into a situation. My father was so quick that at times I thought the conversations he had with people were planned, even ones he had with perfect strangers. I wondered how could he have known what to say so quickly? I would stand in the bathroom while he shaved with that stinky Magic Shave and ask him about conversations that I had heard him have, and how he was able to be so quick-witted. He would laugh and ask me what I was talking about, while basking in the glow of having his young son perplexed by his God-given talent.

As I got older I noticed that I had the same ability to make people laugh, and I was just as quick-witted. The only problem was that I was in elementary school when I found out and I got in trouble many times. But I had that face teachers liked, so they gave me many chances…something I would abuse as I got older. I learned very early that humor was a key to so much: to getting girls, getting out of trouble, winning friendships, being looked at as a leader…hey, who doesn't like someone who can make you laugh?

THE EARLY YEARS

My father was born in Washington, D.C., but raised in Snowhill, North Carolina. He was the second oldest of five kids. After attending North Carolina A&T, he joined the Army. While in the service, he boxed. He was the fourth alternate in the lightweight division for the 1960 Olympics. From him I got the love of boxing.

My mother was born in Nuremberg, Germany, right after WWII. She came from a middle class family, and had three siblings. She hated the Nazis and everything they stood for, and anyone who was prejudiced. She would go on to teach her two kids to not see color. She left home at eighteen years old because of her fierce independence. She worked in nightclubs as a dancer and hostess. She wasn't what you would call a full-out stripper. She wore costumes, sometimes two-piece diamond outfits, and her act including eating fire.

While serving in the Army in Texas, my father met my mother. She was a newly divorced mother of a baby girl. My father told me what attracted him to her was her independence. Back in the 60's, most women relied on men for everything. But my mother was holding it down solo, raising an infant, with her own car, own home and own money. I was born on May 7th in Killeen, Texas (Ft. Hood). Within two weeks I was off to be raised in Germany for the next twelve years with my parents. Life in Germany back then was easy living and being that my father was high-ranked, we lived well. Even though she was married, my mother still did what she wanted to and that was to perform in clubs. The clubs she performed in had well-to-do people in them; women with long cigarette holders and long satin gloves, people drinking champagne…it was a place where men in suits would light women's cigarettes and ask to buy them drinks. My mother loved finer things, from food to cars, clothes, etc. She bought me leather coats and Adidas sweat suits; I ate shark tail soup, Godiva chocolates. I had the best, and I was only seven years old! This is where I believe I got my taste for the finer things.

During summer breaks from school my father would let us stay with my mother as she traveled around Europe to different clubs. There would be apartments above the clubs for the dancers that we would stay in. One night when I was about seven, I wanted some milk and we had none in the apartment. So I decided to go downstairs into the club to see if my mother could get me some. As I opened the back door of the kitchen, I could hear the club jamming and my curiosity overcame me. I slowly slid the door open to the club and saw sex. Not live sex, but sex displayed on a huge screen (back then clubs would show porn movies on big screens) and I couldn't help but stare. The sounds, the movement, the people talking and laughing, looking like they were having a great time. From that moment on, I was hooked. The atmosphere of the club was exciting. I didn't know what I was seeing but whatever it was I was in, sign me up (something I would end up saying many times).

I also loved spending time with my father. He was a slick cat who had a way with words and a great sense of humor. One of my favorite TV shows at that time was *Sanford and Son* and I told my father it would be cool if one day we were like the father and son TV characters. People just wanted to be around him. Being around him made you feel like you were in the presence of someone greater than you. My father read books, traveled the world, wrote poems, wore long minks, and took pictures with guns, posing with some of his Cadillacs. All this from a brother in the Army! Not that it was wrong, but if you looked at an Army brochure, you sure wouldn't have seen his ass up in there! And he was married to a White woman who was his match. Maybe not Ward and June Cleaver, but you couldn't find a better pair.

When I was about ten, we moved to a house that had a club attached. My mother gave up dancing full time in nightclubs and started putting all of her time into opening her own club called *"Why Not?"* (Don't ask me). At the end of the club by the kitchen was a three-room apartment for the waitresses, and many days I would walk by and hear the sounds of sex coming from behind those doors. I would peep through keyholes or windows and see sex, and lots of it. The G.I.'s were getting it in! (No pun intended). Seeing all of this at a very young age would influence a big part of my comedy later on in life.

In Germany at the time, there was only one channel of American TV shows. On it I watched the *Brady Bunch*, *M.A.S.H.*, *Happy Days*, *Laverne and Shirley*, *The Mod Squad*, etc. and then I would go to school and gather my friends around and act out scenes from those shows. This was my first introduction into acting. In school I was a very smart student, but I had to be the class clown. I remember I would have the class laughing and the teacher would get mad and I didn't even care. The attention I received from my fellow classmates was more important than the trouble it might get me into. I just remember all the students wanted to be my friend, and the feeling was intoxicating. I was the leader. Many times I almost got sent home, but no one was home so they couldn't send me there. So I got away with things many times. Thank God, because my parents would have whooped my ass!

One afternoon when I was 10 years old, my world changed. I came home from school to find the whole house ransacked. I mean everything on the floor, and all the drawers in the house pulled out. I got scared and ran to my neighbors' house. They contacted my mother, who was out of town. She raced home, gathered my sister and I and the next thing I knew we were on our way to Washington, D.C. I later found out that my father had been arrested for drug possession.

It turned out he was *"holding"* something for our German nanny and the MP's (Military Police) came to do what they had been waiting to do for a long time—take a successful Black man down. Not to say he wasn't in the wrong, but the way they tore our house up, it was done with a certain air of glee, pride and revenge. That was my first taste of racism. This was the fall of 1978.

THE TEEN YEARS

In D.C., I moved in with my uncle Robert (my father's brother), his wife Pat and her son Craig, who was two years younger than me. We lived in a twelve-story apartment complex. My sister moved in with my grandmother a few floors below us. I went from being protected, to being thrown to the wolves of the inner city. Anyone who has ever grown up in the inner city understands fully well what I went through. But the city makes you tough (sometimes too tough). You lose a little of your purity, kindness, and caring, but you gain a certain toughness you can't find anywhere else. There's no better place to prepare you for what this world is *really* like. "Hood" love is the greatest because if they love you, they *really* love you.

Talk about culture shock. When I went to D.C., I looked like Johnny Mathis' love child, or Prince on his first album cover (long hair, light skin and cute like a girl), which is not a great combination for a kid in *"Chocolate City."* The kids teased me mercilessly and I had no help. My cousin went to Catholic school and I went to public school, so for eight hours a day I was on my own. No one was there to have my back. And looking like a girl made me a target. This was when I began to shape my comedy skills. Up to that point all I knew was I was good at saying funny things. But there's an inner-city skill called **Jonin'** (different parts of the country call it different things like

Baggin', Snappin', Rankin', etc.). It's basically urban slang where one person would talk badly about another, and try to break them down by attacking their looks, clothes, family. Nothing is off limits. It's like street fighting without physically putting your hands on anyone. And I found out I was really good at it. I had a lot going against me, but I had to survive and I found I had a way with words. Whenever someone would try me, I would have a better comeback. I guess all those years of watching my father really rubbed off on me.

My humor was my weapon and I used it like a gunslinger. If anybody said something sideways, that was their ass. And before he or she knew it (that's right, I said 'she'…I didn't discriminate), I had everyone on my side. I started getting a reputation for my **Jonin'**. They used to call me "Lunchbox" because D.C. had a term called "Lunchin," which meant you were a bit crazy. Dudes would try to pit me against everyone, even guys from other hoods. I'm not joking. I was putting much older guys to shame. At this point I started getting an ego. Something that would rear its head several times throughout my career.

As I said before, I was a pretty good student when I applied myself. I once won a Tri-state science fair competition for building a miniature Ford Model T car out of whatever I could find, and because of that I was featured on *Good Morning America* with some other students and a robot. I was so excited. I got up so early to watch the segment which had been taped a day earlier. I was there all day for the taping, but I was only seen on the show for a hot second. So I learned the power of editing at a young age. But hey, I was on TV. Hollywood get ready, *here I come.*

As time went on, and I got a little older, I stopped building miniature Model T's and started looking at miniature female models. I remember the first time I had sex. It was with this girl who was two years older than me, and she lived in the hood of hoods. She called me to come over, saying her brother had left for football practice and wouldn't be back for a while. I knew her older brother and I was kind of afraid of him. I knew if he caught me he'd kill me, but something stronger was calling so that was an ass whooping I'd just have to take. I ran to her house, a trip that would normally take thirty minutes took me only ten minutes. When you've got your 'first taste' on your mind, you find superhuman strength and speed. I remember we got to it pretty quickly on the recliner in the living room. What stood out was that when she took off her underwear, I saw that she had a lot of hair so I thought her punanny was *huge*. See, I only had like three pubic hairs. I kept trying to stick my thing into the hair, and my thing was bending and it was hurting me. Maybe if I hadn't been so busy looking back at the door, I might have been more successful. Then she grabbed it and put it in. I had flashbacks of those porno movies in the club and the sights and sounds I saw at the apartment with the waitresses. I was hooked. Sign me up for real this time! I would sneak over there a few more times. Having sex at a young age made me enamored with it. Some of my funniest jokes are about sex. I always wondered why people act like sex is dirty or wrong, but go behind closed doors and do the wildest sexual things. These people are pure hypocrites. People sometimes would come to me after a show and say, "You're funny as hell, but a bit too dirty." And I would tell them, "I'm cool with that assessment as long as you don't go home and do the same things I just talked about. I'd rather hear someone talk about killing people and then do nothing, than see someone who says nothing and goes out and kills a bunch of people." I love the look I would get from them.

While in D.C. something important happened to me. I became Black. Not literally, but figuratively. I started to understand what it meant to be Black. I was fully treated as if I were Black, by both Blacks and Whites. My eyes were opened to everything that people would associate with Blackness: collard greens, chittlins, rap and R&B music, food stamps, single mothers, weed, nappy hair, big bootys, petty fights, Black love, racism, and I loved it (well, except for the weed, chittlins and racism).

Around 1980 my father got out of prison. My mother came over from Germany and we all moved into a house in Maryland. We moved right over the D.C. line into Seat Pleasant, Maryland, a lower middle-class working neighborhood. This was halfway into my first year in junior high school. Kids in my neighborhood were bussed out to schools where the White kids were, and since I was in a gifted class in D.C., I was put in a high-level class with nothing but White, Asian, Indian and two thick-glasses wearin' Black kids. And yes, I failed miserably. By 8th grade I was out of that level and back around the shit talkers and Joners.

In 1981, I entered high school. I was part of the first class of 9th graders who were starting that grade off in high school instead of junior high. There were 9th and 10th graders coming together. So crews were quickly assembled and since I had a reputation as a good Joner, a few dudes wanted me to hang with their crew. Remember, if you wanted to embarrass someone without putting your hands on them, Jonin' on them would do the trick and at this point I had mastered the quick wit and brutality of Jonin'. You wouldn't believe how powerful words can be, especially at a young age. Every morning before the first period bell rang, a few of my friends and I would sit on a radiator at the end of the hall. The hallway split off to the right and left, so to go to class, one had to either walk down there or walk all the way outside and come through another door. And my crew and I would put a verbal whoop-ass on any and everyone we felt like. I remember I would see people in class that had to walk past us, and I hadn't seen them walk past. They had walked out in the cold and came in through another door rather than face my crew. Even my crew members were afraid to walk off first. We'd damn near have to hear the late bell before we separated. Look, I know what I did was cruel and painful to many students, but back then that's how we played.

I would soon have some pain of my own come into my life. One day after school that same year, I came home to find all the furniture gone. My mother called a few minutes later and told me she was leaving my father and taking my sister with her. She thought it would be best if I stayed in Maryland with my father, knowing I wouldn't like moving back to Germany. My parents soon divorced. I missed my mother, but the thought of moving to Germany overrode any feelings of wanting to live with her. I thought that my father and I would now be like Sanford and Son.

Around this time, Eddie Murphy was all the craze. My friends and I would stay up late and watch *Saturday Night Live*. With me it was an event. After it aired every week, all Black people would talk about for the next few days was what Eddie did on *SNL*. My friends and I bought his first album and listened to it in the basement over and over again. When his stand up special *Delirious* aired, it was a wrap. I knew what I wanted to do with my life—be a comedian. Sign me up.

The high school I went to was a vocational high school (school where you could learn a trade), so on days that I completed projects early, I had time to kill. One afternoon like that, I was in class scanning the weekend section of the local newspaper and came upon an ad for a local comedy club called the Comedy Café. It had pictures of a few White guys performing and of who was coming to the club that weekend. I saw they had an open mic night on Thursdays. I decided after school I would go down there and investigate. I'm gonna be honest (as I have been), I get so tired of comics always saying they first went on stage as a dare from somebody. I'm not saying it ain't true. But did anyone do it like I did? Go there because they wanted to be in show business and become famous?

THE EARLY COMEDY YEARS

I arrived at the Comedy Café in April 1985 when I was seventeen years old. It sat in a little three-story building in downtown D.C., around the corner from the hooker stroll, and above a strip club. Damn, I felt like I was seven years old again as I walked the stairs to the second floor. They had three shows that night. I told the door lady I was a comic who came to watch the show and she let me in without having to pay. The show was already in progress. The club was dark, smoky, and cramped; it sat about 200 people on wooden benches and tables. Ninety-five percent of the people in there were White. There were three performers, a headliner, a feature and an opener/emcee. A Black comic named Kevin was the feature. I watched the show and afterwards, I approached him about how to get into comedy. His words were "write five minutes of comedy and come back on Thursday for open mic night." I said, *"Cool,"* and left. As I got into my car I thought *"what the hell is 5 minutes of comedy?"* I didn't know how to write a joke. I mean, I was good at Jonin' and telling funny stories to my homeboys, but I never timed them. So the next day I bought albums by Steven Wright and Rodney Dangerfield. I took their jokes and made them into Black *"urban"* versions.

I went back the next week, signed up for amateur night at 6 p.m. and drew a number. I saw a young Black comedian about my age; he stood out because most comics were much older than me and White. I introduced myself to him and he told me his name was Martin (Lawrence). I left and went to a Burger King down the block and studied my jokes, line for line. I came back for the 9 p.m. show and sat there watching the comics go on before me. Every time someone bombed, I said to myself "I can do better than that." But when someone went on before me and killed, I thought "what the hell am I doing here?" I remember seeing Martin go up and he killed. I got so nervous because I was going on soon, and as far as I was concerned he was my direct and only competition. The next thing I know they're calling my name, well, sort of. The host said *"Give it up for Piree"* I thought "damn, my career is started off fucked up." I ran up on stage, trying to mask my nervousness with phony energy. I grabbed the mic and noticed everyone staring at me. Just staring. I thought "this is not like in school or on the playground where everyone takes turns Jonin'. These people don't know me." I realized just how long five minutes really is when you're unsure. I went into my first routine and they laughed. I went to my next joke and got laughter again (sorry, this won't be a story where I bombed my first time on stage). I was killing! I ended on a big laugh and said goodnight. I walked to the back of the room where all the comics sat waiting to go on and got congratulations from most of them. I felt like I was on cloud nine, even though those jokes hadn't originated from me. I had put enough of a spin on them, that they were mine.

From that first night I was hooked. A few weeks later I was running late for a show at that club because I got stopped by the police. As I got to the club, I ran on stage and told the story about being pulled over and people laughed. From that day on I got rid of one of those "borrowed" jokes every week until I had my own set of jokes. I started working any and everywhere that had a microphone. I didn't even need a stage. Within two years I had a solid ten minute routine. It might not seem like much time, but to stand in front of strangers and try to hold their attention and be funny for that long, it's a long time. My father wasn't supportive of my career choice. If I wasn't in the house by midnight he would put the chain on the door. I would either have to call my sister and ask her to come unchain the door, stay at my best friend Deryl's house or sleep in my car. Being a young comic, many times meant having to go on late, so I wasn't able to come home by midnight. There were many days when I fell asleep in first period class, because I had been out late performing the night before. I had to make a choice and I chose comedy. But despite that, I still managed to make honor roll.

When I turned eighteen, my father made me go to the Army recruiter. But lucky for me, having been born with only one functioning kidney meant they wouldn't accept me. Back then the military wouldn't accept someone who was missing a major organ. I told my father and his answer was "that's OK, but you're getting out of this house." Like any parent, he just wanted to see his child make it on his own. So I moved out. Now I had the freedom to perform anytime of night. My act grew quickly.

I started bringing my crew with me to the clubs when I performed. We had a few haters, but they dared not say anything. We hung around the killers and drug dealers. We were very popular because a few of my friends would work out dance and rap routines and start doing them right in the middle of the crowd. Especially popular was my homeboy Deryl. He could rap, dance, do impressions, voices and Jone. I believe he could have been a star if he hadn't let so many things sidetrack him. To this day, people still talk about him or ask me about him when I go back home.

As I look back, Washington, D.C., was both a fun and dangerous place in the mid 80's. Speaking of dangerous, the night of October 4, 1987, I almost lost my life. My crew and I were hanging out and before going out on the town, we decided to stop at McDonald's. After going inside, we decided to go to another burger spot across the street called Roy Rogers. We walked back through McDonald's to get to our cars. As we exited we were right by the drive-thru lane and this car almost hit us. Now you have to understand, I rolled with dudes that didn't have a problem with slapping up a nicca (I spell this word with c's to soften the blow). So words were exchanged and the car pulled over to the parking area we were in, followed by another car load of people. They exited their cars and I could tell by their accents that they were Jamaicans. That meant nothing to me, they were a bunch of clowns who were being disrespectful and they needed to be dealt with.

One of them told the two cars to leave, and he and two other dudes stayed behind. But every time we threw our hands up to fight, they would back up and just talk shit. After a few minutes, I could tell they didn't want to fight, so I tried to get all of my boys back into our cars. But every time the last person got in the car, they would try to open the door. We'd get out ready to fight and they would back up some more. I remember getting in the backseat and yelling to my boys "Let's go, fuck them clown ass niccas." I looked out the back window and saw some more Jamaicans running back over to their homeboys' rescue. So I knew it was on, time to put in some work. I got out of the car and stood in between my boys, when I heard someone say "Burn 'em." I then heard what I believed was a starter pistol. Up until then I had never heard a real gun. I had only heard gunfire on TV. Deryl yelled "Oh shit!" and ran forward between the cars. He had gotten shot in the leg. I panicked and ran, still not fully understanding what had happened, but by his yell I knew it wasn't good.

As I was running, I felt a shock like electricity hit my lower back. I thought the dude had hit me with a stun gun. Then my wrist exploded. I looked at it and all I could see was meat and blood. I knew something was wrong but I still couldn't grasp the moment. Then I got shot in my leg and ran right out of one of my shoes. People wonder why I didn't fall, but when you have that much adrenaline pumping in your body, it sometimes won't let you fall. I ran around the back of the McDonald's and towards some woods about twenty yards away, and saw Deryl hiding in them. I started yelling at him for not getting into the car. I couldn't run anymore, so Deryl put me on his shoulder and carried me across traffic. Cars swerved around us but did not stop. He dropped me on the median and we sat there as cars blew past us. He eventually attempted to take me back to McDonald's, but they had locked the door on us and called the police. I started crying because I thought I was going to die. I thought if you get shot, you die. I really didn't know anyone who had gotten shot and lived. When the ambulance came and took me away, I asked the paramedic if was I going to die, and he said, "Naw, yo ass gon' be alright." After that, all I could think about was where was my other brand new New Balance 995 shoe? They cost $130. Remember, this was 1987!! I gave up hanging in the streets after that and started focusing on comedy. My homeboys really encouraged me to pursue comedy and stop hanging out so much and that's what I did. This episode in my life would become one of my more famous comedy routines.

Around this time I saw Tommy Davidson and Martin Lawrence go off to Hollywood and start tasting success. I figured if they could do it, I could too. My manager at the time, Ron, used to work with Tommy and he suggested that he and I go to Hollywood to see Tommy film the first episode of a new show called *'In Living Color'*. So in the summer of 1989, we headed to Hollywood. When wc arrived, I remember how clean Los Angeles smelled. You can smell the ocean air, but if you stay there long enough that smell dissipates. It was better than I imagined. There were mountains next to the freeway, palm trees, and beautiful people. We decided to walk around Hollywood. All I could think was that we were official. We were really in Hollywood. I thought I would see stars walking around; everyone I saw I'd stare at, trying to figure out which star they were. These were normal people, but to me they had to be someone. Hell, they were in Hollywood. Normal people aren't in Hollywood, only stars right? The next day we went to watch Tommy shoot his new TV show. Now I didn't really know him, but we had crossed paths in D.C, a few times. I put on my best "going-to-watch-a –TV-show-taping-and-I'm-the-next-star-from-D.C." outfit. I think it had polka dots of different sizes. Don't act like you didn't have something with polka dots in your closet in the late 80's...remember when plaid, stripes and polka dots some how matched? Well only if you had on patent leather shoes.

We pulled up to the Fox studio lot and drove up to the man at the gate. He had us sign in and gave us a parking slip and told us where to park. I was so excited. This was the big time, the real deal. We got to go into Tommy's dressing room and wait for him. As I waited I thought one day this was going to be me. Tommy came into the room full of energy. He offered us anything and everything in there. Tommy showed me love as if he had known me forever. He is a lot like me when it comes to D.C. comics. We just have so much love. Tommy has such a carefree spirit. I was nervous for him, but he acted like none of this fazed him.

Then Martin came in and I was excited to see him, because we had a little more history. I always felt I was on his heels when he left D.C. But the rhythm between us wasn't what I was expecting. Not to say it was bad, but I've grown to know Martin. He will only give you what he wants you to have. I heard he is really a cool person once you get to know him, but I've never gotten to *"know"* him. We chopped it up for a minute, and Martin and Tommy both told me to leave D.C. for good and come to Hollywood because this was where I needed to be. And at that moment I decided that within a year, I would be in Hollywood. And if I say I'm gonna do something, it's done.

It was time for the taping, so we grabbed our seats in the audience. For the first show, they did sketches of Mike Tyson on *Love Connection*, Men on Film and a few more. During set changes, Tommy would come out and entertain the audience. He did killer impressions of Sugar Ray Leonard and Sammy Davis, Jr. He had the crowd eating out of his hands. Another cast mate would take turns. A white guy named James Carrey (before he *became* Jim Carrey). He would contort his body and do outrageous moves. After the taping, we went upstairs for a little post-taping celebration. I couldn't believe my eyes, standing there was Robert Townsend (he was hot off of *Hollywood Shuffle* and directing Eddie Murphy's concert film *Raw).* I asked him to take a picture, which he did (funny, not knowing one day I'd be working with him. He directed me in *B.A.P.S*). We said our "hellos, great show" to the cast and left.

That night we were going to the hottest Black comedy club in the nation: the Comedy Act Theatre (CAT), the house that comedian Robin Harris built. When we got to the club, it was already sold out. I saw a D.C. comic named Buddy Lewis out front, who told me they weren't letting anyone else in. I was going to straight bum rush the door and get in. It would be a chance to see Robin! At the time, he was the hottest Black comic. He had appeared in *Do the Right Thing, House Party* and was being touted as the *next* Black comic. I told my manager Ron I was going in, sold out or not. But he told me to get back in the car and he'd work it out. A few minutes later he came back to the car and told me we couldn't get in and that we'd try another day. I told him I wanted to go in now, fuck next time, and we got in a big argument (when I was young, if I wanted it I had to have it). We never went back on that trip and Robin died a few months later. I never got a chance to see the great Robin Harris live.

Two days later I returned to D.C. more determined than ever to get back to L.A. and stake my claim. I had given myself one year to return. Things started looking up for me. BET asked me to be a judge on their new game show called *Tell Me Something Good*. This would be my first real national exposure. I remember we had a studio audience and after the first taping, a group of girls asked me for my autograph. My first taste of being a star. I counted down the days until I would leave for the West Coast. I worked construction jobs, I built decks, did anything that I knew I could easily walk away from. See, in the D.C. Metro area, most people wanted a government job that they would do for the next twenty years, and complain about for the next twenty-five years. But there was one thing in my life at that time that wasn't so easy to walk away from. Around that time, I had met a woman who would later become my wife. But I *had* to walk away. I was ready. I was supposed to move out to L.A. with Kevin, the comic I met when I went to my first comedy club. We were going to stay at some friends' house for a few weeks and then get an apartment together. We had become friends, and everything seemed good until I saw him on the Friday before we were supposed to leave. I said, "I'll see you Monday morning for our three day drive to L.A." He told me he wasn't going. This is where my young cockiness served me well. I said "OK, I'm still going, with or without you. You're not going to stop what is my destiny."

In September 1990 I had saved up $1,100. I took whatever personal belongings I could stuff into my car (a 1983 Nissan Pulsar) and headed for Hollywood. A funny little story: I had packed my car to the limit and discovered while driving that I had packed away the box full of all my cassettes too deep in my car. The only two cassettes I had out were from the groups BlackBox (remember the song *"Everybody, Everybody?"*) and Soul II Soul (*"Back to Life"*). Well I heard those whole damn cassettes for three long-ass days; I don't think you understand. The *whole damn* cassettes (laugh). Now whenever I hear songs from those albums, I break out into *hives*. Naw, those songs hold a special place in my heart. They remind me of the young free spirit I had.

THE EARLY HOLLYWOOD YEARS

I arrived in Los Angeles on September 5, 1990, ready to take on show business. One of my manager's friends let me crash in his two bedroom apartment with him and two other guys. I slept on the floor on an air mattress for the first six months. To make money, I took any crappy job that came my way. I first worked as a phone reservation agent for an airport shuttle company, then as a bank teller, and at night I would hit up every open mic spot around L.A. My name started getting some attention.

In 1992, I got a call from Michael Williams, the owner of the Comedy Act Theatre. Michael told me that a producer was interested in seeing me showcase for a new show called Def Comedy Jam (DCJ). One of the talent scouts named Bob Sumner came out from NYC to see me perform, and afterwards he booked me on the show. The next thing I knew, I was heading to New York City to do DCJ; it was unreal. I flew with a few L.A. comics: D.L. Hughley, Simply Marvelous, A.J. Jamal, etc. We stayed at the Millennium Hotel in Times Square. I was so excited when we received a package in the lobby containing our credentials and a per diem (spending money).

The night of my taping we went to the Academy Theatre in a van. I remember we got out of the van and had to walk past hundreds of people in line. These were New Yorkers, so there wasn't a smile in the line, plus it was freezing. I had heard how tough N.Y. audiences could be. If you weren't funny they had no problem with letting you know. New Yorkers relish that reputation. I remember thinking that I had to go on and do my act as quickly as possible so the N.Y. crowd wouldn't *boo* me, so I did my act at warp speed. I had a good set. If you ever see me on that show, you can see how fast I was going. One of my signature routines came from that night: the "being shot at McDonald's" bit.

Once my DCJ show aired, things really started moving. I was getting booked at a lot of places, but the money was still small. I hated working as a teller. Any true artist hates doing anything other than their art for a living. Customers recognized me from DCJ and they would literally let customers behind them cut in front of them and wait for me to be done so they could be my next customer. I was getting more stand up work, but I would have to make up excuses to get off work at the bank. I believe my grandmother died three times in eight months, and always on a Friday or Monday. Hey, you gotta let someone get out of work if their *Grandma* dies.

One day, everything came to a head with my branch manager. I was called to her desk right before I was about to get to my station. You know a bank manager's desk is usually right behind the tellers, out in the open. I sat at her desk and she asked me, "Do you want to work here or do that comedian thing?" I could feel some of the other tellers listening. All of the frustrations, the lying, and begging to take days off got to me and I said, "You can kiss my ass!" I swear it was like an out of body experience and I could see myself sitting there. She said, "Excuse me, what did you say?" I said, "You heard me, you can kiss my ass!" I got up and walked past all the tellers. It was like something out of *Jerry Maguire*. I went downstairs, collected my jacket, and my brown lunch bag that contained Oodles of Noodles, an apple, a couple of cookies, and a juice box in it. Hey, times were tight. I walked back upstairs, and the branch manager was standing in the doorway with her arms folded. I gave her a look that said, "Bitch you'll be here the rest of your shitty life." I got in my Pulsar, drove to my one room apartment, pulled out my futon, sat there and said to myself, "*Pierre, if you're going to do it, this is the time.*" Truth be told, I wasn't even scared. I was more relieved than anything else. I haven't had another day job since.

Now that I could be a full time comic, my act started really developing. I was invited back to do Def Comedy Jam again in 1995 and had a great set, and that's when things really took off. My wife and I had a daughter, Bianca, that year that I was crazy about, and I doted over her; if you saw me, you saw her. I split my time between trying to be a great comic and being a great father to her. I took my responsibility as a father very seriously. She would get whatever she needed: love, attention, whatever. Now my wife, not so much. In my own stupid way, I thought that since she was an adult, she didn't need that much attention. You'll never hear me say I was a great husband. A great provider, yes, but not a great husband. Fellas, let me tell you, women are just little girls grown up and they need the same attention and love that you would bestow upon a little girl. If you don't take anything else away from this book, and if you want a happy relationship with a woman, remember that.

THE HOT YEARS

Robert Townsend would come out to the local comedy clubs looking for the next talented comic who might be making noise. One night at the CAT he had his female assistant, Charlie, approach me after I had gotten off stage to tell me that Robert wanted to meet with me in the back. I couldn't believe it. All of the other comics noticed this and kept their eyes on the situation. Robert told me he liked me and he was working on something that I might be perfect for. He got a brief history on me and thanked me. I saw Robert at various clubs around town for the next few months, him always telling me he has something for me. I started thinking he was full of shit. But six months later he called to give me a part in the movie *B.A.P.S.* After filming *B.A.P.S.*, I landed another movie role in *How to Be a Player.* Soon after, Dr. Dre tried to sign me to his label *Aftermath*. The deal was $15,000 for five albums. With all that money he made off The Chronic album, I thought he could've thrown a young brother some mo' money! I thought his ass must have been *smoking* some Chronic! But he's a businessman, I can't be mad at him for that.

I was swept up in a whirlwind of change. Money started coming in from touring. I was invited everywhere and I went. I went from doing everything by myself to having a manager, agent, lawyer, trainer and publicist. Sony wanted to sign me to a holding deal. That's where a company has the rights to an artist, meaning that for a certain amount of time, the artist can't do anything unless it's for the company or they approve of it. They wanted me for a year at $200,000 and I said no. I had friends at the time who were getting deals three times as big, and I thought I was worth at least that. They came back and offered $225,000 and I still said no (I told you I was a little cocky). I told them that they would have to have a bidding war for me with Fox, Warner Brothers, NBC, and I would be showcasing my talent at the Comedy Store. They called my management and begged them to get me to sign, because they didn't feel like being part of that bidding war and didn't want to send their writers to the club. I was in the office when my manager took the call. He looked back at me holding his hand over the phone, asking *"what do you want to do?"* I said *"tell them no, and to meet me at the club."*

That night at the Comedy Store, none of the reps from those different companies wanted to sit anywhere near each other. It was so childish. It was a Wednesday, which is not a hot night and I did my set. I knew it wasn't one of my best, but I did well. The next day, Sony pulled their offer from the table and no one else wanted to do a deal with me. They said they didn't see a TV show in my future. Say goodbye to $225,000. Damn!

Al Haymon (a major concert promoter) offered me a holding deal of six months for $75,000, in which I had to host the *Budweiser Super Fest Tour (BSTF)* for thirty dates. I happily took this one. I didn't want to keep turning things down. Plus I had to start thinking about my family when I made decisions. But it was too late for that, my newfound fame had taken a toll on my marriage and in a few years it was over. I started traveling more and more. I took care of my family financially, but I wasn't emotionally there for my wife. I thought if I bought her things and she really didn't have to worry about money that I was doing my husbandly duties. But I wasn't being a good husband. Your spouse needs time, not money.

I was working a lot, but I wasn't getting in any movies. I was close to getting parts; I was close in *5th Element* and *Jackie Brown* (Chris Tucker got those), *Blue Streak* (Dave Chappelle got that), and *Next Friday* (Mike Epps got that). I was never mad at any of them, hell, we're in this business to work, not watch others work. By 1999, I was getting frustrated with the business. I was getting close on movie roles but not landing them, and the demand on the street from people wanting to see me in another movie was taking a toll on me. It made me wish that I could make one of my own scripts into a movie. Finally a role came up and I took it. It was with Leslie Nielsen (*Naked Gun* fame), called *2001: A Space Travesty*. It was only paying $50,000 and I'd have to go to Germany and Canada for twelve weeks. But with the money I was making I could shoot one of the scripts I had written and see where that might take me. I didn't really enjoy working on that movie; they held me back from what I do best and that's being *funny*. But hey, I needed the money. When I got back from filming, I took that money, plus $20,000 out of the $25,000 I had in my bank account and decided to shoot one of the scripts I had written: *For Da Love of Money*. My wife was supportive of this. I only had fourteen days to get it done. Two weeks! I know it's crazy but that's how I lived. I had the best time I have ever had on a set, even with the pressure of getting it done on a shoestring budget. The cast, crew and I had a blast. The movie made it into theatres, which is amazing, then went on to make millions on DVD (which I saw none of) and has had a successful run on BET. One day I'll tell you how I *really* made that movie with tricks, lies, begging, borrowing, and stealing. Ok, ok. I'll tell you one story. In the movie, there is a scene where I break the inspector's car window with a brick...what really happened was that I rented a car for $30 a day, with a $9 a day insurance policy. We only needed the car for one day. We actually broke the window, took the car back, and being that I had the insurance; I paid nothing for the damage. So the stunt cost me $39. When someone comes up to me and tells me they like that movie I light up inside. Even if you don't like it, you have to applaud my effort. I'm more proud of that movie than anything I've done in the business. It's not about how good or bad it is, it's the fact that I did something that people didn't think I could do.

During the next few years, I saw the best and the worst of people. Those who were willing to do anything to make it. I saw desperation, fear, greed, and bold-faced liars—and that was just in my inner business circle. The desire to make it in this business many times comes before common sense, morality or logic. Most people in this business are crying inside. There are people who are reading this right now, who know what I'm talking about, but are too afraid to do the right thing for fear of failure. I don't blame them because they have to deal with their own demons on their own time.

Despite the success of *For Da Love of Money*, the money I was making wasn't enough. My agent dropped me, and my manager stopped calling me. I didn't find out why my manager stopped calling me until two whole years later. I always carried a dislike for him for that. I thought of the many times he begged me not to fire him, so for him to go out like that and not even be man enough to tell me he didn't want to manage me anymore, I thought showed what a weak man he really was. My lawyer, publicist and I went our separate ways.

I was one funny, frustrated, fragile, fucked up comic.

THE REBUILDING YEARS

By 2002 I was divorced and tired of Hollywood, and decided to move away and get my senses and life back in order. I moved around for a few years, before settling in Phoenix, Arizona, where I stayed for three years. While I was away from Hollywood, people on the street would still come up to me daily and tell me how much they loved my comedy, how they enjoyed my movies and wanted to see me back on their TV. So I decided to move to *"Black Hollywood,"* Atlanta, where I could start training my funny muscle again. And the city embraced me. Every time I was out, someone wanted to hire me for something.

I know I'm not as hot or new as I once was; hell a lot of comics have had slumps, Chris Rock, Eddie Murphy, Jamie Foxx, so at least I'm in great company. But the one thing that I am is FUNNY; that has never left. I'm funnier now than I was before because now I have more to talk about, and I'm not trying to keep up an image. I have nothing to prove. And when a comic is fearless, he truly becomes great. I still work on the road all the time. But for my fans, I will get back on the big screen. I owe it to you.

Looking back over the years, I regret putting my wife through some of the things I did. I regret many things about who I became. Don't get me wrong, I wasn't a bad person. I just lost focus on the man I knew I was. I cared about things I shouldn't have and didn't care about things I should have. I wouldn't encourage anyone to get married before you understand what it means to be married. Especially if you want to be an entertainer. It's far beyond sharing bills, and taking care of the other person financially. Your heart, mind and soul have to be in it. And this business can easily separate you from your partner if you don't truly want to be married. Look, I know people who can't keep a marriage together and they both have nine-to-five jobs and live in "Your Town" USA. Now throw in what I just finished talking about... Good luck!

I also don't ask for forgiveness. I was who I was. And at the same time, I don't seek forgiveness from the people who did me wrong. This life is what was dealt to me and I played the hand I was given. As I said before, life throws you many curves, it's not the curves people notice as much as how you straighten them out.

I decided to straighten out my future by looking into my past. One night I was on stage performing in Atlanta and someone yelled out, *"How was it working with Halle Berry?"* And I told them the truth. Someone else yelled out, *"What kind of dude was Tupac?"* And I went on to explain my experience with him. Before I knew it the audience was asking about so many celebrities, and I tripped out realizing how many I knew. On my way home I decided it might be cool to write about my Hollywood friends, so here it is.

This book was written without malice, discontent, hatred or revenge, but I do tell it how it was, and I tell how these events went down to the best of my honest knowledge. So sit back and enjoy.

This is why I had to learn to Jone...

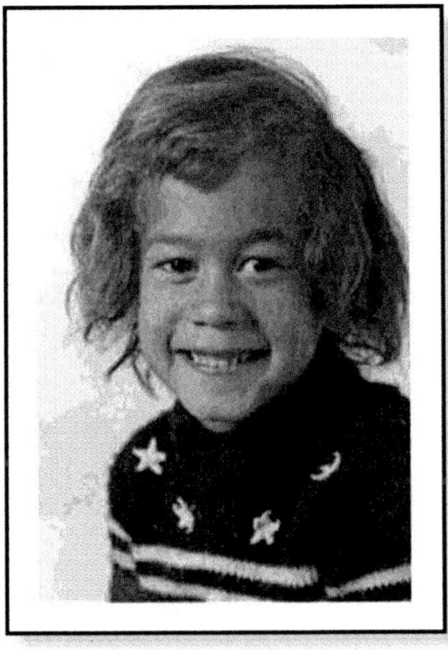

"What illegal sweatshop did they find you in?"
"You should be singing 'I got the Golden ticket'"
"Negro take off that wig!"
"What's up with the Michael Jackson chin implant?"
"Is that a partial bang?"
"You got the face of Human Trafficking"
"You looked like you auditioned for Garanimal commercials"
"You look like a girl"
"Yo momma don't know how to braid?"
"You Mexican?"

"You look like an underage porn star from the 70's"
"You looks like Princess Lea and Lando Calrisian's love child"
"Madame CJ Walker would be proud to know that the straightening comb and/or perm was put to good use"
"That green jacket says 'I like sunshine and rainbows and boys'"
"You look like Johnny Mathis' stepson"
"Man.....was you the first nigga to get a Just For Me perm?"
"You look like Farrah Fawcett and Keith Partridge had a baby"
"That green corduroy jacket is so tight it looks like a big ass tattoo"

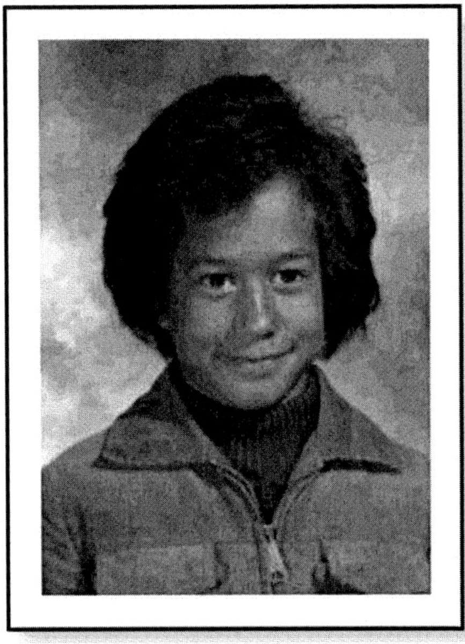

Age 16: Can someone say "Employee of the Month"

"Please understand this was the 70's"...

"Everybody in the DC area has a picture of themselves against a wall..."

Age 20: "I don't know why I had a ring on my wedding finger. Look at that suit! Miami Vice had nothing on me"

"This is me getting my Grown Man on. But where's my belt? And look at the pinky..(laugh)"

Age 17: my first week on stage

On the set of
For Da Love of Money

Directing on set:
"The most fun I
ever had on a
movie set"

My Road Dawg Joe P. and I: On the set of *For Da Love of Money*

T. Rexx: 1997 in Cancun, Mexico. "Whatever happens in Cancun STAYS in Cancun".

Oh Hellll Naw! My first trip to LA in 1989. I needed my ass beat for this outfit. What's worse...my socks or Ron's short-shorts? Man Rule #21: "Never put yo arm around a man wearing Biker shorts!"

"YOU ONLY LIE TO THOSE YOU FEAR"

-John Gotti

P.S. I fear no one.

Aaliyah *(Singer)*

It was August 1997 and I had worked out a deal with music promoter Al Haymon, who now manages boxer Floyd Mayweather. He wanted to be in business with *me* so he offered me what is known in the business as a "holding deal," meaning that he had the first rights to me (well, my talent) for future projects for an allotted period of time. Part of the deal was that I would host the thirty-city *Budweiser Superfest* musical tour.

Our first city was Buffalo, NY, where we played a 15,000-seat venue. About an hour before the show, I noticed a group of dancers in the hallway. Suddenly, Aaliyah appeared from her dressing room. I was stunned by how small she was, but, at the same time, how pretty she was. Her skin was flawless. As she joined in rehearsal with her dancers, she seemed very happy. But I can't lie, as I watched her, all I kept thinking was, *"This is the young lady that R. Kelly married?"* At the time, she was 21, but she looked younger than her age. I couldn't tell if she was mature in other ways. She was beautiful, just not in a womanly way.

Today, she is generally loved and that's taken for granted. It wasn't always like that in the beginning. I remember a few times when she performed and her voice was a little too angelic for the size of the venues, and the crowd would "boo" her. Smartly for her, she had Kid Capri deejay between her sets. She would do a couple of songs and the "boo birds" would start. Before she closed her set, she would do a costume change so Kid Capri would spin for ten minutes and then she would come back for two more songs. Aaliyah handled the audience reaction like a pro. She never seemed to let it bother her.

Many nights I would see Aaliyah sitting on the floor of the hotel hallway after a show, talking to Ginuwine, her dancers and back-up singers. I felt she had a big sense of family and really wanted her touring experience to feel like a family trip. I believe Aaliyah's father was her road manager; and he made sure that everything stayed in order. He would stand at the elevator doors in the lobby and ask any young girl that he didn't recognize how old they were and who they were coming to see. If they weren't at least eighteen, they weren't allowed to go upstairs. I thought that was cool because he cared enough to make sure no one got into trouble.

Aaliyah would sometimes bring these two people on stage and introduce them as her producers. Now, I'd never heard of any artist bringing up their producers on stage during their performance. After a few cities, I wondered, "*Who in the hell are these people?*" So I went backstage after one show and there they were just *chilling.* So I asked them, "Who the hell are y'all?" They introduced themselves as Timbaland and Missy Elliott. I hit it off with Timbaland and his bodyguard. I couldn't believe this nicca had a bodyguard! He wasn't even famous back then. Timbaland is a cool dude but he was always worried that I might Jone on him.

When the tour finally ended, I ran into Aaliyah backstage and she gave me the biggest hug and told me she would love to work with me again. Within a month of that tour, I would see Aaliyah, her back-up dancers, Missy and Timbaland on many different videos. After the tour, it seemed like every time I turned on the TV, a video would pop up with someone I knew from the tour. I started getting into watching videos really closely just to identify back-up dancers.

The next time I saw Aaliyah was at the premiere of Spike Lee's *He Got Game.* Aaliyah and I were hanging out, doing press when she spotted me and gave me a big hug and kiss. We talked for a moment and said how much of a blast we had on the BWSF tour and said we'd stay in touch.

A few months later, I was home watching TV when I got a call about a plane with Aaliyah on it that had gone down in the ocean near the Bahamas. When you're in show business, you get news so fast. They weren't sure then if she or anyone else had survived. Often times, these are rumors, so you try not to jump to conclusions. I made a few calls and no one had heard of anything. I turned to MTV and they weren't reporting anything either so I hoped maybe it wasn't true. But my source was really in the know, so it stayed in the back of my mind. I went to a comedy club that night and I started hearing about the crash but the details were still sketchy. A few of the comics there confirmed the facts and details. My heart sunk. I had to walk away and just be alone. I thought of all the times I had seen her on stage, backstage, running in the hallways, eating. Just every moment I had ever seen her.

I would never say that Aaliyah and I were great friends or that I knew her very well. Still, I was very hurt by her passing. All I could think about was that the great potential and sweetness she possessed was lost forever. God has a plan and it's not up to us to understand it. We can only go along with it.

A side note: Two, young male hairstylists who worked at the same place I got my hair cut also died in that crash. I didn't even know they knew her. I didn't find that out until BET did a documentary a few weeks later.

(See photo in insert)

Allen Iverson *(Basketball Player)*

In 1997 my career was in full swing. I was performing a sold-out week at a comedy club in Philadelphia. One night my good friend Dakota, who's from Philly, took me out to Gotham, a local nightclub that was hot at the time. We got to the club and were taken to the VIP section. In there, I spotted a crowd of about ten guys at the bar and in the middle of them, I noticed Allen Iverson. His height, or lack thereof, immediately stood out to me. He was about six feet and I'm about an inch taller. Seeing how short he was gave me more respect for what he was able to do on the court. To be that height and dominate in a sport of men who are normally at least 6'6" or taller, that's impressive. I started thinking I could play pro basketball.

All the women around him trying to get his attention also stood out. It was like a game of Double Dutch, one woman would come into his inner circle to talk to him and the next woman would wait for her turn. As soon as the other woman left, another one would jump in the circle.

I went over to pay my respects. When he saw me, a big smile covered his face. His homeboys tried to mean-mug me like they were protecting their food source. Come to think about it, they were. He started telling his boys what a funny dude I was. It tripped me out that he knew me so I hung around a little longer, hoping to catch one of those girls jumping in and out the rope. Just kidding. After a few minutes, I parted ways because it was becoming too much with that group.

The next time I ran into him, it was a year later. We were in Cancun, Mexico. My cousin T. Rexx and I were hanging out for spring break. We used to wear these really bad looking fake teeth and would make people die laughing. One day, T Rex and I were hanging out in front of a club, holding court. We had the crowd laughing and Allen and his homeboys (Allen never traveled with less than three guys) came over dying laughing. Allen has a good sense of humor. T Rexx could do all sorts of voices with those teeth, some of the funniest stuff I've ever seen.

Later on that night, T. Rexx and I were walking in front of a few clubs and Allen saw us and begged us to put in our false teeth and start clowning. Right behind him, about six feet back, five girls were following him. When he stopped walking, they would stop walking *but five feet away.* When he started walking again, they would too. Like a mother duck and her ducklings. T. Rexx and I would make Allen laugh every time we put those teeth in. As we started to talk about me coming back to Philly, gunshots rang out and it was every man for himself. I didn't see him anymore on that trip.

I saw him once more in Denver, at the 2005 All Star Weekend, in the lobby of the hotel where I was picking up Gabrielle Union and her girls. He and I had short words and he still asked me about them teeth. I bet you, even today, I could still have A.I. laughing if I put in those teeth.

Andrew Dice Clay *(Comic)*

Around 1996, I was becoming hot news in L.A. and The Comedy Store was like my home away from home. One night I was scheduled to go on after Andrew Dice Clay performed. Since there was no host, comics would bring each other up. So, after you finished your set, you brought up the next comic. Well one night, Dice had to bring me up. Instead of just bringing me up, he decided to extend his act. "Who's next*?"* he asked, and someone yelled out, "Pierre. He started going in: "Pierre? Who the fuck is that?" A magician? (Pause) OK, some guy name *Peeee* Air."

Now, ya'll know me by now, I'm from D.C. I don't give a fuck about no star. If you disrespect me, I gotta let you have it. He called me up there like I was a nobody. I don't give a damn if I was at that point or not. I didn't take shit off **No One**, including Andrew Dice Clay. So, I went on stage and said: "Give it up for the Italian Stallion…Andrew Silverstein (his real name). He ain't even Italian, he's Jewish!! And I heard the crowd oooh and ahhh.

I performed for ten minutes. When I got off stage, I was ready for the asshole to approach me. He said nothing and just walked by me. You've got to be careful how you treat people. You never know who'll write a book. Of course, he would never remember this incident. I was so 'beneath' him at that time.

Anthony Anderson *(Actor)*

I met Anthony in 2003 at the Improv on Melrose, one of L.A.'s hot comedy clubs. He had done several movies and was receiving major love in the club. He was standing in the hallway that led into the showroom with a mutual friend, who introduced us. From the jump, I felt he was a cool ass dude. He knew my name before our friend finished introducing us. That surprised me. "I know Pierre's funny ass," he said.

I had no idea he was from Compton. I congratulated him on his success and he did likewise. He was just as you see him on TV or in the movies—fun and likable. He doesn't make you feel like you're in the presence of a major urban star, which I can respect. He lets his work speak for itself. We had a few more words and we parted ways. A few years ago, when he was accused of sexual assault on the set of *Hustle and Flow,* I really couldn't believe it and was truly happy when he was acquitted. His star was rising and I hate it when a young artist doesn't have the chance to reach his full potential.

He also likes to Jone, but he don't want no parts of this. I'd eat dat ass up... When we see each other now, he always wants to Jone with me. He's gotten pretty good too. I hear he's doing stand up. He's someone who can easily transition into stand up. Anthony's the real deal—a very good actor and a person you'd want to have in your presence. He's definitely someone I would like to act with. I think we'd both bring some craziness to the screen.

Arsenio Hall *(Late Night TV Show Host)*

I performed on *BET Comicview* in 1992. This was at a time when I had a little chip on my shoulder. See, I had done *Def Comedy Jam* on HBO and I felt like I wasn't getting the respect I deserved. Bernie Mac, D.L. Hughley and Bill Bellamy were getting movie parts and were on the road with Def Comedy Jam's comedy tour and I thought I was just as funny as them. You gotta understand that by that time, I had been in the game for seven years and was mostly performing in White clubs where I had witnessed unfunny White comics working for years. I felt like I had paid my dues. So, if I viewed you as someone who wasn't helping Black comics or me, you were going to hear it from me.

At this time, *The Arsenio Hall Show* was hot and an appearance on his show could set you apart from the pack. He would have some unknown comics on his show once in a while but they were always White and I kept thinking, *"Why won't a brother help his own?"* Well, when it came time for me to tape *Comicview*, I was going to let the world know what Black comics had been saying for the past few years amongst ourselves (I know I was a cocky little son of a bitch, but you know how I do).

D.L. Hughley was the host that season and he called me to the stage. I did my act and things were going well and the crowd *loved* me. And now for my grand finale: I did an unflattering impression of Arsenio (long finger and all). I turned my back to the audience (like some magician), slipped this long plastic finger on and turned back around and was in full Arsenio mode. In Arsenio's voice,

I said, *"Sandy do you know who those people are over there (pointing to the imaginary dawg pound)? Those are young Black comics who need a break, but I won't put them on my show. Ahh yes, yes."* People were laughing and in shock at the same time. I felt like I was **king** when I walked off stage. All the comics backstage loved it.

Word spread throughout the Black comedy scene. People couldn't believe I had the heart to say that, no less on national TV. But I was young, cocky and naïve about the business. I didn't mean any harm. I was just trying to change something that I thought was wrong. As I gained more years of experience in the business, I began to realize how hard it is to get people on a show, even when your name is on it. I started regretting doing that because I'm not a mean-spirited person, maybe a little crazy, but I really do try not to have any malice in my heart.

One night a few years later, I was at The Comedy Store in Hollywood, years after Arsenio's show was off the air, and ran into him for the first time. I asked if I could I speak to him and I apologized for doing that joke. He hadn't seen it or heard about it but he told me if I could have reached him, he would have loved to have had me on his show. True or not true, he was cool and after I apologized I felt better. I shouldn't have slammed another Black comic for something I didn't understand.

Baby ***(Rap Mogul)***

In 2000, I was staying at this nice hotel in Atlanta with twenty floors, where the balcony is inside the building, and you could look down to the lobby. I was just getting off the elevator and I saw Baby of Cash Money leaning over the balcony, just looking down. Their music was just beginning to take off so I knew who he was and went over to him to show love and maybe talk about some future projects.

I had just finished my movie *For Da Love of Money* and felt I could talk to him on a business level. Maybe some soundtrack work. He knew who I was and gave me my props. We talked for a minute and it was time to exchange numbers. He turned his back and yelled to someone in his room to take my number. He told me to go into the room and give his girl my info so I went into his suite while he stayed outside.

This young lady came out of the bedroom with his phone and, fellas, when I tell you she was fine, I mean she was fine! I was like "DAMN I got to own my own record company." All I could think was, *"Dude when you fall off, she's gone."* Come on ya'll, he ain't gonna make the cover of *GQ Magazine* any time soon. But, then again, I guess anything is possible.

We never did business together, but, through the years of seeing him move in the industry, I've come to the conclusion that that girl was lucky to be fucking with him.

Babyface, Me'Shell Ndegéocello *(Singers)*

It was Sept 5, 1996. It was the night of the Mike Tyson/Bruce Sheldon fight in Las Vegas. It was also the same night Tupac got shot. That's the reason I remember the date. Benny Medina, who has managed Will Smith, Tyra Banks, Jennifer Lopez, P. Diddy and, oh yeah, me, had a fight party at his house.

I drove to his house in the Hollywood Hills. It was small but tastefully done. As I entered, I noticed Benny had some major players at his house: Me'Shell Ndegéocello, Babyface and some other producers. I ran into Me'Shell right when I entered the house. She was hot off her first album. She was really down to earth. What stood out about her, besides her shaved head, was how flawless her skin was. She's a beautiful woman. Many men and women judge women by their hair. To me, a woman doesn't need a weave down to her ass to be defined as beautiful. Tell me Erykah Badu and Amber Rose aren't beautiful women! I found out we were both from DC and even knew some of the same people and had performed at some of the same spots back home.

When I sat down next to Babyface, I was a little star struck. It tripped me out how he looked exactly like he did in his videos. His skin was smooth, his hair was perfect and he had some big ass white teeth. I can't tell you how many people look way different off camera. Not Babyface. He was camera ready. I was waiting for a camera crew to pop up and start filming. We had a nice conversation about my career because I had just wrapped up two movies. He was a very nice guy, and really down to earth. I was taken aback by how normal he was. You gotta understand I wasn't used to being around many famous people on his level at that point in my career. I know of many people on his level who won't even give you the time of day.

The fight came on, and was a first round knockout. Since it was still early, I went to The Comedy Store and hit the stage. I later learned the news about Tupac.

Bernie Mac *(Comic, Actor)*

In the summer of 1994, I was the featured act for Bernie at a theatre in Fayetteville, North Carolina. Surprisingly, this would be the first time I'd meet him. Of course I knew about Bernie before I ever met him. Like many of you, I remember Bernie from *Def Comedy Jam* when he delivered his infamous line "*I ain't afraid of you mahfuckas.*" Like all great Hollywood success stories, there's a great back-story about how that moment came about.

Whenever comics taped *DCJ*, we were told there would be five comics taping but only four would air; so, whoever didn't rise to the occasion, wouldn't be airing. Talk about pressure. (FYI: ya boy taped twice and aired twice, "Thank you very much.") Well, the night Bernie delivered that famous line that catapulted him to *"ghetto super stardom,"* a comic from D.C. went on before him and got his ass handed to him. That young New York crowd booed and heckled him, even gave him the silent treatment. You name it, they did it. Bernie, being the veteran he was with seventeen years in comedy at the time, was next and watching from the side of the stage. He went out there and flipped the script and told that crowd *"HE wasn't afraid of them."* And the rest is *DCJ* history.

But back to me meeting Bernie. Show time was fast approaching and the theatre was filling up, but no Bernie. I heard Bernie had missed his flight because he or someone in his crew tried to board the plane with a gun, and the next flight wouldn't land until after the 8 pm show time. Because Bernie was now scheduled to land at 9 p.m., the promoters stalled the show until 8:30 p.m. Even then,

Bernie had to come straight from the airport to the theatre. The promoters came to my dressing room and asked if I could perform longer. Now, I only had about thirty minutes worth of good material and fifteen minutes of bullshitting material. I told them that I just didn't feel comfortable or confident with doing more time and then they sweetened the pot with a bonus. "Oh more time? No problem. I got this"

So the show started and after ten minutes, the emcee called my name. I went on stage a little nervous because mentally, I hadn't prepared for anything more than a twenty minute routine and I didn't know how long I would have to stay on stage. It was kind of like walking off a cliff blind folded; only I didn't know when the drop was coming. But I *killed.* They loved everything I said, except for one joke. That night, I learned a big lesson.

See, in my first *DCJ* appearance, I did a joke about being shot at McDonald's which the public *loves.* (YouTube it if you don't believe me.) Most people didn't realize I really got shot at McDonald's. I used to feel once I did a joke on TV, I wouldn't want to do that joke live anymore because I felt people had already heard it. Who wants to hear a joke when you already know the punch line? But then again, people watch the same movie over and over again and already know the ending. People like what people like. Well, I was on stage this night and a man in the audience kept yelling out *"do the McDonald's joke"* between each joke. I tried my best to ignore him, but he was persistent. After a while, I couldn't ignore him anymore. So, I stopped my act and said "OK, you wanna hear it? Here it goes." And I did the joke with very little energy and emotion. When I got to the punch line, there was nothing, no real laughter. The lesson I learned that night was, don't do a joke if you're not going to commit to it.

Anyway, I got back to my planned routine and I saw the promoters giving me the light to let me know Bernie had arrived. I had done forty-five minutes and except for that little *blip,* I rocked the house. Walking off the stage, I was so proud of myself for conquering such a major challenge. I got backstage and I saw Bernie with his entourage. Bernie was wearing a tracksuit, looking like he truly had *just* gotten off a flight. He thanked me for holding it down and I thought, *"Let's see you follow that!"* Yeah, I was a little full of myself. I grabbed a seat in the audience. Bernie walked on stage and his big stage personality just took over. Within minutes, he had them eating out of his hands. I thought to myself, *"This man had no time to prepare or get his head together, not even a chance to change into his performance outfit and he has this crowd eating out of his hands."* About five minutes into his act, he stopped and said, "You don't understand. I ain't afraid of you mahfuckas" and the crowd lost it. I guess he could follow my little bullshit act . . .

From that day on, I realized you give the crowd what they want, not what you want them to have. If there's a joke they love, you give it to them and give it to them like it's the first time they've heard it. People come for those jokes. Each time you come to a city, add a few new ones, but keep a few classics. When Bernie finished that night, he got his well-deserved standing ovation and was off. I didn't see him anymore that night. Later on I would see Bernie around, but I never shared the stage with him again.

The next time I ran into him was on the set of *How to Be a Player.* We did *B.A.P.S.* together but didn't share the screen. On the set of *HTBP* he was really down to earth, cracking jokes. His stardom was rising so fast, but he seemed unaffected by it. He truly didn't have an air about him like he was above anyone on the set. People felt like they knew Bernie, even White folks. He was always smiling.

Whenever he performed in L.A., I would come out to support him. He was always kind to me, even in the midst of everyone around him—fans, agents, managers, other celebrities—he'd make it his point to speak to me, even if only for a moment. I tried to open up for him on one of his tours and he'd always say we would but it never came to pass. The lessons I could have learned touring with him.

Like so many others, I was saddened by the news of his passing. I had known he was sick for awhile, so it wasn't a major surprise. But what I can say about him, and this is no Hollywood B.S., is that he was a true talent and truly one of the good guys in this business we call comedy.

Bishop Don Juan *(Pimp)*

I was backstage at the Universal Amphitheatre for the *Master P's No Limit Comedy Jam* show in August 1999, talking to a few of my friends when I spotted something green and shiny in a crowd of people. After careful examination I noticed it was Bishop Don Juan, standing next to Snoop Dogg. I had seen him before in videos and on HBO's *Pimps Up Hoes Down* documentary. It's one thing to see a nicca on TV dressed like a pimp with all the gold jewelry, but seeing one LIVE is a trip!

I approached him and introduced myself. I explained to him that I was in the process of shooting a film, *For Da Love of Money*, and would love to have him in it. He was cool as hell. He has an air about himself as if nothing or nobody bothers him. All I could think was, "I'm talking to a real live ass pimp. Not an actor dressed up, but the real deal". He gave me his personal number which surprised me, because he didn't really know me. I told him I would contact him soon with the details of the film.

A few weeks later I called Bishop and asked to meet with him to talk about the role. He invited me to his home, which happened to be three blocks from mine. As I pulled up to his apartment I noticed a money green older model Rolls Royce trimmed in gold, that matched exactly what he had on at the concert. I thought, *"Damn, this nicca might have a car for every outfit"*.

I knocked on his door and was taken aback a little when this fine young Black woman opened the door and walked me to the living room. She told me Bishop would be out in a moment. The living room was covered with memorabilia of his legacy, from awards, to newspaper clippings, trophies (how does a nicca win a trophy for pimpin'???), pictures, etc. But never mind all that; all I could think was, *"Who was that fine young lady? I know she can't be with him!"* (I didn't respect the game at this point). She looked like she was 26 years old, and Bishop had to be at least sixty years old. All I can say is "*Pimpin' ain't Easy!"*

Bishop entered from a back room wearing slippers and a robe, looking like a Black Hugh Hefner. But I really tripped out when I found out homegirl *was* with him. I described to him what I wanted him to do in the film and told him there wasn't much money in it. He was cool with that and said he'd see what he could do.

The timing was off, and it didn't work out for Bishop to be in *For Da Love of Money*, but I came away from meeting him with a newfound respect for him. From that day on, whenever I would see him in public I would always drop to one knee as I shook his hand, paying homage to a cool ass Kat.

I ran into him backstage in Detroit while he was on Snoop Dogg's *"Puff Puff Pass"* tour. I told him we would do business one day. It's crazy because whenever I'd see Snoop, Bishop was right there.

On February 14, 2003 I was in Chicago at the Regal Theatre starring in the play *"Something He Can Feel"*. Who was sitting in the front row in all his Pimpdom? Bishop. After the show I ran into R. Kelly backstage, but I heard Bishop was in the lobby so I had to go out there and pay my respects. As usual when I saw him I dropped to one knee and shook his hand. He was flanked by a few fellas, who are also "pimped" out. One guy in particular caught my eye, because he had on a floor length white mink coat. Damn that shyt was sweeet. I said my hellos, and they told me how much they loved the play. Just then my best friend, Joe P., called me away because it was time to get on the bus to go back to the hotel. Bishop, his crew and I parted ways.

I got on the bus, and within seconds I heard gun shots ring out. Everyone ducked and scrambled for cover. Cast mates started running onto the bus, and we sped off to the hotel.

News of the shooting started circulating, and people started saying that Bishop was shot and killed. After all the smoke cleared, it was discovered that the dude in the white mink was shot a couple of times while sitting in the backseat of a car next to Bishop Don Juan. The shooter was only after the dude in the mink; they say he walked up to his side of the car and unloaded. That was the last time I saw the Bishop.

Brian McKnight *(Singer)*

In the summer of 1999, I was in Boston, participating in a celebrity basketball game at a local recreation center. When I got there, I was immediately ushered into the locker room in the gym and had to get dressed next to Brian McKnight. Now, I had seen him before at other celebrity basketball games I played in, mostly at Magic Johnson's "A Midsummer Night's Magic" charity game, but he was never on my team so we didn't have any real interaction. I had never spoken to him before. I only saw him on the court shooting around. He seemed way to into playing, like he was trying out for the NBA or something. I think he plays in a celebrity basketball league. Honestly, I did these events just to have fun with the games and the fans. I did notice that he wasn't that outgoing with the fans.

Well here in Boston, we were on the same team so that was the first time we came into real contact with each other. I was in the locker room with everyone, laughing and clowning like I like to do, but Brian was just sitting there getting dressed, very much to himself. Now, I like the people around me to have a good time so I said something to him but he gave me a "I'm-too-focused-on-this-game" look. I don't know if he felt like that or not, but that's how he looked. One of the organizers came in and said some winners of a contest were waiting to meet the stars and get autographs. But when I turned around, Brian was gone. Being that I love the fans, that meant more time for me to spend with them. We're here for these folks. I know that some celebrities take these games way too seriously. It wasn't the NBA Championship. It was a charity game!

I have a different impression of him since that day and I would go on to hear that he was arrogant from many others. That could be heresy. I have never understood how artists can't take the time out for a few fans. Without them, you'd be back to shopping your demo. But I will say that Brian is a very good basketball player. I see he works on it a lot. Now, in all fairness, he may have changed since then. I haven't seen him since. I'm still a fan of his music but if the heresy is correct, next time I will bootleg his shyt…(laugh).

Bruce Bruce *(Comic)*

I first met Bruce in 1994 when he was the host of one of the stops of the *Creative Tour,* a 10-city comedy tour through the South. This stop was at a notorious club in the hood in Atlanta called 559. The club was so bad and so rowdy that the headliner, who would usually do 45 minutes at all of the other clubs, was told to just do ten to fifteen minutes. This club had it all: dope dealers, hoodrats, real killers, weed smoke, and it was packed beyond capacity. You know, a normal Black club. Have you ever seen a club so bad that police would be both inside and outside, and they were afraid? If a fight broke out there, yo ass was on yo own. But they loved Bruce up in there. He held his own. Hell, he probably went to school with half of them.

I survived the only two times I did that club, but only by the skin of my teeth. As soon as I felt I was losing the crowd I would say, “good night”. So I gained Bruce’s respect because like I said, many comics who went on to fame and fortune had gotten their ass handed to them in there.

Bruce and I co-headlined a tour throughout Ohio in 1995, meaning we would take turns following each other. I remember on that Ohio tour how hard Bruce made it for me each time I had to follow him. But it made me stronger. We would do a show and the next day get in the little ass car of the cheap ass promoter. Bruce was much bigger at that time than he is now. He would sit in the backseat and I sat in the passenger seat, with the shyt slid all the way up! Let’s say I was damn near in the glove compartment…(laugh)

We would stop off for breakfast before we left each city. Bruce would eat a BIG breakfast, and we would pull off. A few minutes later we would stop by a gas station to get gas and Bruce would get out and grab some snacks. I thought, *"We just ate ten minutes ago!"* He came back looking like he had gone grocery shopping. Milk, Ding-Dong's, cookies, chips, etc. The he would proceed to get busy in the backseat! We stopped for directions at a gas station a little later and Bruce had to get a little snack, something to hold him over for lunch or dinner.

Once we got to our hotel, we checked in. And a few hours later I would come down into the lobby and see Bruce in the restaurant eating!! I can't lie; I thought he was going to eat himself to death. I was worried for the brother. But when show time came, Bruce would deliver the goods. One thing I liked about Bruce was his likability. Young or old would gravitate to him. His humor was easy on the ears. When he was on stage, you felt like you were in the presence of a family member. C'mon now, we all got someone in our family like Bruce Bruce.

We have worked together many times since. We even worked together in the movie The *WASH.* Bruce is that fun guy many people think he is. I admire the success he has had even though we went down similar paths and he became more successful as a comic. But I don't have a hating bone in my body for Bruce. He did what he had to do to get where he is. I truly enjoy working with him. To this day, Bruce Bruce is the same person I rode in that car with in Ohio back in 1995.

Cece Peniston *(Singer)*

By 2005, I was really fed up with Hollywood, so I moved to Arizona and bought a house. To keep my comedy skills sharp while away from Hollywood, I started a talent showcase on Sunday nights at a club called Jackson's On Third. There was a talented young singer who would perform there every week, who I befriended. He later told me that Cece Peniston was his sister. I've always been a huge fan of hers, especially her song *"Finally,"* So I told him to invite her down. Sure enough, she came a few weeks later. I noticed her sitting in a booth next to the stage, and was taken aback by how pretty she was in person. She had lost a lot of weight from what I remembered. After the showcase, I sat down and struck up a conversation with her. It was refreshing to see how sweet and humble she was. She told me she was working on a new album and that she believed this release would put her back on top. For some reason I believed her. We talked and hit it off like old friends. I dug how carefree and down to earth she was. She would end up coming out to my showcase many times. She would always tell me what a huge fan she was of my comedy. It feels good when other artists tell you they are fans of your work, because most don't want to express their like for other artists. Well, at least the ones who aren't secure in themselves don't.

A few years later, while I was living in Atlanta, Cece was in town and called me up, inviting me to grab a bite to eat. She said she was in town shopping for a record deal. As we drove to the restaurant she played me her new music for me. Folks, when I tell you the stuff was hot, I mean the stuff was *hot!* I asked if I could keep a copy, and I tell you, I listened to that CD for weeks straight. I hope she reaches the same level of success she once had. Even though she had a pop hit, she can really sing.

Cece Peniston- "Backstage at my concert in Phoenix with one of my favorite people"

Cedric the Entertainer *(Comic, Actor)*

It was mid 1995, and I was touring throughout the south on the *Creative Comedy Tour.* This tour went through ten clubs, in ten cities, in two weeks. Each club would see a new rotation of comics per week. It seemed that in almost every city I was performing in somebody would ask me if I knew Cedric the Entertainer. My first thought was, "*who the hell is so bold to call himself 'THE Entertainer'?*" But everyone was telling me how funny he was. He had done the tour a week earlier so I was following him. When I was young and trying to make my way in this business, I didn't wanna hear about another comic arousing so much attention. Especially from the people I was trying to impress.

A few months later I was taping BET's *Comicview.* It had turned into a competition, and the winners would get a half hour special. I got really close to getting one. In fact, at the BET Comicview Awards that year I received an award for being, let's say, "cheated" out of getting a special. The award was called "The Best Stood Up Stand Up Comic" Award. But all of the talk was about Cedric. So when it was time for him to film his special, I went to check him out for the first time.

When he came on stage, I wasn't impressed by his initial look. He was kind of fat, dark, had on a cheesy suit, and wore glasses. This was not the "Cedric the Entertainer" I had conjured up in my mind. But once he opened his mouth, I understood. He rocked the house and he was easily the funniest comic that year, including me. He just connected with Black folks in every way with his jokes; from church, to singing, to doing impressions. He wound up becoming the new host on *Comicview* after D.L, Hughley, which was a great choice. I would see him around and he'd always call me Grandmaster P.

In the summer of 1999, I was in Montreal, Canada filming *2001: A Space Travesty* and Cedric was in town hosting the Urban Night at the Montreal Comedy Festival. Many comics have gotten discovered at this festival, and went on to major careers. On this particular night the lineup was set and the room was packed. I wanted to see if I could slide on stage, even though I wasn't an invited guest of the festival. I was trying to get in front of a particular big time agent. My manager went backstage and asked Cedric if I could perform. He came back out and said, "I think he'll put you on." I went backstage to thank Ced and he told me "I'm gonna put you on because of you, not your manager, because I don't like him." My manager was White and at times had a way of rubbing Black people the wrong way. I ended up leaving him a few times because of it, but my loyalty kept bringing me back.

When Cedric did that for me, I officially had love for him. It's funny; I've worked with almost everyone except Ced. But I can tell you he's just as likable in person as he is on stage. Cedric is one of my favorite comics.

(See photo)

Charlie Murphy *(Comic, Actor)*

I first met Charlie at the Uptown Comedy Club in Atlanta in late 2009. He had two big nights there. I had heard about him doing stand up, but the word was that he wasn't that good; not only from other comics (they can be haters), but from audience members too. I wanted to see for myself before I passed judgment. I was a huge fan of his work on the Chappelle show, plus he had my homey Freeze Luv opening up for him.

I have a weird feeling about entertainers, i.e., rappers, actors, etc., who get into stand up comedy. Comedy is not an easy thing to do. It may look easy, but trust me, it's not. I think your chances of success are better if you've come up through the ranks of comedy clubs. Many times entertainers decide to do stand up and people flock to see them only to find out they're not funny. It leaves the audience with a sour taste in their mouth, and then when a good comic comes to town, they won't come out and support because they got burned the last time. But hey, who said show business was fair?

I got to the club and Charlie was already on. I missed Freeze. Charlie was doing better than I thought he would be. He tells long-ass stories, but funny and interesting shit you don't usually hear at Black comedy clubs. I thought he did a good job but the wait staff wasn't too crazy about him, and some of the audience members weren't either. But I wouldn't say he bombed by any means; many people did like him. But I now understood why some people didn't think he was funny; it's because he doesn't do the traditional "hood" humor. I respect him for staying with what he believes in, and not changing what he knows. When it comes to Black folks, our expectations are ridiculously high. If they're paying over $20, you better be on some Super Hero of Comedy level. Times are too hard to give away hard earned money on some B.S. One reason I love Black audiences though; they *will* let you know if you're good or not. White folks let a lot of mediocre shit hang around. They say Black folks don't really support. They do, just nothing mediocre.

I went backstage to see Freeze and Charlie after the show. It's always good to see Freeze; he always keeps it 100% real. That's why Eddie Griffin and Charlie take him on the road with them. You need real people around you when you travel. I introduced myself to Charlie. A couple of things stood out about him. One, I was surprised to see that he wasn't wearing as much jewelry as I had seen him wear in magazines before. That nigga used to keep more jewelry on than a kiosk in the mall. And two, his *big* ass white teeth. You look at him and you see darkness, and teeth. I wouldn't say we hit it off. But he was cool and likeable. I can tell he's guarded. That happens to people who find new fame sometimes. He ain't Eddie Murphy's brother anymore, he's Charlie Murphy now. So I can imagine how people are coming at him. I decided to play it cool. After I bought his book I got a better understanding of who he was. Charlie Murphy is the kind of guy I could see myself hanging out with. He's real, and he knows his place in the business. Charlie is going to be alright in the stand up world.

Chris Rock *(Comic, Actor)*

My road manager, Joe P., and I first ran into Chris sitting at a terminal at the Los Angeles airport in 1996. This was right before his HBO special *Bring the Pain*. Chris was sitting *by himself.* I found it kind of strange that someone on his level was traveling solo. I mean he had been on *SNL,* in movies and on *In Living Color.* Hell, I had someone rolling with me and I was nowhere near being on his level. What else tripped me out was how skinny this dude was. I know I was skinny but damn, I had him by at least twenty pounds!

I have been a huge fan of Chris's stand up for years. If there is anyone I see myself as wanting to be on par with, it's Chris. The way he breaks down relationships, politics and does it with a bit of a bite. That's right up my alley. At this time, he had just gotten off of *SNL* and wasn't the hottest comic in America, as he would become. I asked him where he was going and he said he was headed to perform at a college. I was struck by how shy he seemed and how he didn't give much eye contact; he seemed to be uncomfortable in public settings. Some celebrities are like that, i.e., Michael Jackson. We exchanged a few more words, then his flight was called and he headed to his gate. Joe and I went to our gate.

A few years went by before I saw Chris again. One afternoon I was walking across Robertson Boulevard in Beverly Hills, where many upscale restaurants line the street. I was on my way to a lunch interview at a popular spot to eat called The Newsroom. I saw this guy come running across the street towards me, his clothes looked shabby, teeth looked bad, and his hair was nappy. I reached into my pocket thinking this was a homeless dude needing a dollar or two. But as he got closer I realized it was CHRIS ROCK! I thought this nicca was auditioning for *New Jack City 2*! Now, he had done two HBO specials by this time, so I was taken aback by his appearance. I said "What's up?" and he said "Hey Pierre, how are things?" I said "Good" and he walked past me. I was surprised he knew or remembered who I was. Even though I have been in a few films, I'm still surprised each time someone famous acknowledges me. Even though I know I'm one of the funniest comics in the country, I still sometimes felt beneath many comics because they had more money, fans and fame than me. As Chris walked away, I couldn't believe someone with that much money would look like that. But some artists are just about the work and not their image. Or maybe, I caught him on a bad day in Beverly Hills.

He has since fixed his teeth and now is looking like new money (damn, I need a HBO special!). I can honestly say as a comic, he's one of my favorites. He has great material and delivery. He came to the Uptown Comedy Club in Atlanta in 2008, which surprised me because it is an all Black comedy club and I knew he had graduated to theatres and mainstream comedy clubs. But he was working on material for his upcoming HBO special. Now I could have gotten in for free, but I had a date with me and since I liked Chris, I paid the $45 per ticket to see him. There ain't but two or three comics I'm willing to pay to see; but being a fan of his, I had no problem paying.

The club, which holds four hundred people, was packed that night. The audience was almost equally mixed with Black and White people. All I could think was Chris was really famous, because he got White people to come to the hood. His opening act, Mario Joyner, was good, and had clever material. Then it was time for Chris to come out. The electricity in the room was ridiculous. Chris just walked out, no fanfare, no intro song, no nothing! Of course the crowd went wild. Not Black crowd wild, but White crowd wild, standing, clapping, and whistling. Black crowd wild is a different kind of Wild. You get the standing, clapping and whistling, a few shouts of *"motherfucka you better be funny," "damn you fine,"* a few *"I love you's,"* a drink bought up to you...then, silence. Now you *better* be funny; you've got a two joke maximum to get funny or you're gonna hear it from a nicca in the audience who thinks he's funnier than you. But there's nothing like Black crowd love when they love you. It's pure. Because they know what you have been through to reach that moment, coming up amongst black folk. And they figure that if you made it to the top, then you've been through some shit. It ain't an easy ride growing up Black.

So, Chris went into his routine. I could tell he was working some things out. Comics know when other comics are on point or just winging it. I'm glad you fans don't. There have been many of nights I had to wing it. But the audience never knew and that's all that mattered at the time.

Two minutes into his act Chris saw me and gave me a shout out. Again, I was taken aback that he would acknowledge me. I watched another hour and decided to leave, because I know Chris; when he is working a routine out, he can do two hours of performing. Plus I was on a date and had some unfinished business to handle. When I see Chris now on magazines, hosting shows, and doing specials, I'm envious. I probably shouldn't be; they say "with much gained, much is asked." I still think he's one of the best out here.

Chris Tucker *(Comic, Actor)*

One of the first places I got paid to travel to and do comedy at was the Comedy Act Theatre in Atlanta around 1991. It was owned by Michael Williams, who also owned the one in L.A. This is where I met Chris Tucker. He went up on stage, and I won't even front. The energy and charisma he had was off the charts, even though he only performed for five minutes. I knew then a star had been born. As soon as I got back to L.A., I told Michael Williams that there was this young comic named Chris Tucker that was fire. And every time I would go to Atlanta to perform, there he was. He would always ask me how it was in Hollywood, and tell me how badly he wanted to go out there, but I think he was still in high school then. Less than a year after I saw him last in Atlanta, he was in L.A.

I remember one night in the summer of 1993, I was driving down the Sunset Strip in Hollywood headed to the Comedy Store and saw Chris waiting at the bus stop. So I gave him a ride to the club. After I finished my set, he asked if I could take him home. I took him to the apartment in Hollywood he shared with another comic. When we got there, I had to use the restroom so I went upstairs with him. He opened the door, and I saw there was no furniture. I could tell it was a one bedroom apartment. I heard music coming from the bedroom, so I asked him where he slept. He pointed to a sleeping bag in the corner with a little lamp and a few books.

After that I couldn't help but watch his career take off. It went so quickly. A lot of comics hated on him, because he didn't have much material, yet he was getting work everywhere. I always felt there is no order to success. Success comes when it comes, quickly for some, longer for others and never for many. You are the only one who can truly judge your success. One day Chris showed me a newspaper clipping of a tour we were on together with some comics who had gone on to successful careers. Chris wasn't even the top draw on this show, but the article had only his picture in it, taken from the show while he was on stage. It talked about how the show was great, but how Chris stood out. When people are talking about you and you ain't even the main dude on the show, it's just a matter of time. I knew Chris was about to leave us comics behind.

One time I was on tour with Chris and I remember he had this script for an Ice Cube movie called *Friday.* He had to fly back to L.A. to audition for it. I didn't think much of it. Hell, I auditioned for things I didn't get. I told him good luck. As we all know, he got the part. During the filming of *Friday*, I heard Chris was killing it. I missed the screening of the premiere, but I went to the after party. At the party *all* I heard about was that Chris was going to be a star. We all know what happened after that. I would end up going up against him for a few movie roles that I got close to getting, but they always went to Chris. It got to a point that I jokingly told my agent, if Chris is up for the part I don't want to audition. But I will say he did a great job in every one of those movies, so I couldn't be mad. They weren't meant for me.

I've seen Chris many times since those days. I even had Thanksgiving dinner at his parents' house in Atlanta (I see why he became a comedian, his whole family is funny). Whenever we see each other now, he always asks what I'm working. He's still a fan of mine, like I am of him. I sometimes smile when I see him being treated like a big star because I can still remember him as a young amateur comic asking me, "*How is it in Hollywood?*"

(See photo)

Charlie Wilson *(Singer)*

It was early 2003 and I was in Little Rock, Arkansas, rehearsing for a play called *Something She Can Feel.* Joe P. and I were in the lobby checking into our hotel when Charlie came in with an older Middle Eastern woman. When he enters a room, a lot of energy comes with him. You know Charlie's in the house. He was wearing a tracksuit and a whole lot of jewelry. I thought someone was shooting a 1985 rap video in the lobby. I was a fan of the Gap Band in their day so I knew who he was. The woman who came in with him checked him in, so I thought she was his assistant. He came over to where I was sitting and started talking. I found him very down to earth and he seemed to love to laugh. He was a star amongst us so-called stars and he seemed to be happy to be with us. Let me tell you, I know some artists who haven't had as much success as he has, who think they are doing you a favor to be in your presence. I can't stand them assholes and they know who they are.

One day during lunch I found myself alone with him. By this time we had built a rapport. He told me some things about him coming up in the business, like how he and Rick James did so much cocaine in the early 80's (cocaine is a hell of a drug), some of the parties they attended and sex that went down in those days. He told about the money he blew and how he found himself broke, without a dime. He had gone to rehab, and when he got out NO one was there for him. They gave him the clothes he had worn in there and sent him out. Not home, because he didn't have a home, but just out the door. The woman who ran the rehab gave him some money and a place to stay, to help him get back on his feet. He wound up marrying her, and that was the woman he was with when I first met him. She gave up running the clinic to handle his newfound career. He had to start from scratch after his last stint in rehab. Now when I see Charlie, I'm so happy for him after all he's been through. Charlie is a good dude, so support him when you can, because I do!

One of the things that stood out about Charlie and that tour was his cologne. I asked him, but forgot what cologne it was. But that shit was fire. I ain't gay but I really wanted that cologne. Another thing was, Charlie was *always* chewing gum. He had more gum than the candy lady in the hood!

Now every time I run into Charlie at a show, he always reminds of the good times we had during that play.

Dr. Cornell West *(Professor, Speaker)*

In the spring of 2007, I went to Diddy's restaurant, Justin's, in Atlanta. I went with a female friend to see what the food was all about. As we were seated at our table waiting for the waiter, I saw Dr. West at a table a few feet away, sitting by himself. This is a cool cat. He rocks a suit and scarf, has the nappy afro, the 1970's beard; I dig his style and free spirit. I told my friend who he was and she had no idea (look, all my friends aren't worldly. With me, the bigger the booty, the lower the I.Q, can be). I told her I was a fan, and she said "Thank you and I like your comedy too." I said "Girl, not yo ass. A fan of Dr. West". (Did I tell you she had a big booty?) I love people who speak their mind and fight for a cause. So many people do just enough to get by, never getting in harms way. They play it safe and complain about why things are the way they are. This man tries to get Black folks to expand their minds, past what the system wants us to do. A lot like I do on stage. I decided to pay my respects. I went over and thanked him for what he was doing and was ready to just hear him say "Thank you." I started to walk back to my Big Booty, I mean, Friend. He said "Young brother, I like what you're doing also." I was thinking *"Man, you don't know me,* "but then he said, "You're a funny guy. Keep telling the truth on stage, I like what you're doing." I was speechless. This man actually knows me? I asked if he was in town for a speech and he told me he was visiting his son at a nearby college. I thanked him again for his work and headed back to my friend. The One and Only Dr. Cornell West knows me and likes what I'm talking about on stage. Nobody can tell me shyt! And I've become a bigger fan ever since. If he's on TV, I'm watching. Thanks Dr. West.

Oh, yeah, the food at Justin's? Skip it. Sorry Diddy!

Dave Chappelle *(Comic, Actor)*

I first met Dave at the Comedy Café in D.C. around 1988. He was too young to be in the club, so his mother would have to sit in there with him in order for him to perform. I always thought he was a really good comic, even at seventeen. I remember being envious of him because White people really liked him and the older White comics would take him around with them to open for them. Back then there weren't many Black clubs in D.C. to perform in, so it was either perform at White clubs or one of the two Black clubs in the city. I never hated on him. I just tried to act like he wasn't on my level because he was younger than me; I was twenty at the time. I tried to write him off, but he was too good.

He moved from D.C. to New York a few years later and was off to the stars. There was a comic named Tony Woods in D.C. that people say Dave stole his style from, but having seen them both from the beginning, I don't believe that. I just believe they both have similar laidback styles, and Dave just took off first. Since Dave knew I was friends with Tony, I always felt when I would see Dave he never truly embraced me fully. This hurt back then because I always felt pride for any comic from D.C. who was doing well in show business. I would see him at comedy clubs in L.A. and we would have idle bullshit conversation for a minute and go our separate ways. I remember one night I ran into him and his writing partner, Neal Brennan, at a nightclub in L.A. and they told me they had just sold a movie script they wrote called *Half Baked.* I was kind of happy for him. I mean, I *am* competitive.

The next time we crossed paths, it wasn't on a personal level. It was for a movie part that we were auditioning for, and the director had narrowed it down to Dave and me. I thought this is my chance to step up to his level. He had been in a few more movies then I had at that point. My manager told the director would make the decision over the weekend. Monday came and I got the call. I hadn't done well enough and the director went with Dave. Damn, damn, damnnn! The movie was *Blue Streak*. When it came out I went to see it, and Dave did an excellent job. At that point, I wasn't mad; at least one of my D.C. homies got it. Since then, I haven't seen Dave in years but I have watched him grow into a great comic. I was sad to see the things he went through in the last couple of years, but I wish him nothing but the best. He'll always be my D.C. homie.

David Allen Grier *(Actor, Comic)*

I first met David at the first taping of *In Living Color* back in 1989, but we didn't really speak. I was an 'unknown' and he was starring on a new show. I became a fan of his after seeing some of the characters he played on *In Living Color*. My favorite movie role of his was the part he played in *Boomerang*. But the next time I caught up with him was in 1997 at a boxing gym in L.A. where we both were working out. A lot of famous actors would work out there, but they never wanted to get into the ring. But David liked getting into the ring and I was always willing to get in there with him. So we boxed a few times. David can actual box pretty well (especially for an actor, because a lot of those dudes are "candy asses") and I would always try to push him. He wasn't one of those *"please don't hit me, but let's box"* types. We had some pretty good battles, to the point that the gym owner would pull out his camcorder. What I wouldn't do to get my hands on those tapes, just in case David can't remember how I put them things on him!

I haven't seen him much since the gym days, but I see he's doing well. David is a cool guy. In fact, I bought his biography. I thought maybe he'd mention some of the ass whoopings I gave him (laugh).

DJ Pooh *(Director, Music producer)*

I first met Pooh at an audition for *The Wash* in early 2000. He was the director and writer of the movie. I came in and he told me he was a big fan of mine. I was a fan of his music production. He did a few of Ice Cube's classic songs, i.e. *Who's the Mack.* Many people don't know that he wrote the movie *Friday* with Cube. He was actually supposed to play the part of "Smokey," but it ended up going to Chris Tucker. As I got to know Pooh, I could see Pooh's comedic influence all in *Friday*. I didn't get the part in *The Wash* I went out for, but he was such a fan, he wrote me into the film (remember the "attempted leather suit" scene?). During breaks in filming, I was Jonin' on George Wallace (he's good at Jonin'). He wasn't ready for a fool like me. I tore him a new ass during the breaks. We should have put some of our battles in the movie. Pooh heard about some of the shyt I was saying from other cast members, so he wanted to put me in more scenes. But they had a tight deadline and never found the time. I think as far as street comedy goes, Pooh is really underrated. He could have tried his luck as a stand up comic. He knows comedic timing. Think about his performance in *Friday,* nobody runs away like that after getting their chain snatched. Pure comedy.

After filming we would talk about me about helping him on future projects. He had some great ideas. But trying to connect with him is the hardest thing; he's all over the place. One day I heard he was at his baby momma's apartment. My best friend stayed in the same building. So I drove over there and sat on some steps out of his view and waited for him to leave. As he walked out I called him. I watched him look at the phone and push 'Ignore' and as he walked past me. I said "Oh, you can't take a nicca's call?" He started stuttering (which he already does), and all I could do was laugh. No hard feelings. We've talked several times since then. I wish him all the luck. Pooh truly has talent.

DMX, Redman & Method Man

(Rappers, Actors)

It was a cold night in D.C. around the fall of 2000, when I first met DMX, Method Man and Redman. I was in town hanging with family, and someone had invited my cousin T. Rexx (who's also a comic) and me to a studio to watch a live taping of a BET hip-hop game show. I think it was my boy Tigga. I was in the hallway chilling with producers, P.A.'s and backstage people, just laughing and eating all the craft service food (ain't nothing Hollywood about me). All of a sudden this entourage came through the hallway. It was DMX walking a pit bull in the damn studio, with ten motherfuckers around him! I was thinking, "Damn, I know this nigga ain't got a damn dog inside this TV studio!" They ushered all of us into the same dressing room because they were about to let in the studio audience. When we got into the dressing room, it was me, DMX, his dog and like three of his boys. His other boys were guarding the door and running errands. He turned to one of his boys and said "find me a little shorty that would come in here and suck my dick." Damn, it's like that? Shit, make that two! (Just kidding) I decided to leave; not because I'm afraid of "head," but because more of his homies came in and I didn't know them niccas.

So I left to find another dressing room to chill in. The next door I entered was Redman and Method Man's dressing room. What stood out most were all the free clothes in there from Russell Simmons' Phat Farm line, and boxes of new Timberland boots. They were just piled up on the floor in the corner, we're talking at least twenty outfits a piece. I started thinking about what I was going to steal (sorry, it's the D.C. in me). There were about four people including my cousin in there. I had been a fan of those two dudes for a minute. They were like the Laurel and Hardy of rap. When I entered they showed me love. We joked around for a minute, and then someone wanted to Jone. I think it was Method. Now you know that was right up my alley. Method struck first, talking about my six month old Timberlands, and my jacket that was a few years old, but nice. And Redman was laughing and co-signing, like friends are supposed to do. Now I have never been at a loss for words, but I looked at Meth with all his new shit, then I looked at Red with his new shit…do you know how hard it is to talk about dope, new shit that you want? I had to take it to their physical appearance, but it was a moot point. It looked like I was reaching. They got me that night. As you can see I've never forgotten that night. There haven't been too many times when someone got the best of me. I've made dudes walk away, or even want to fight me from Jonin'.

The next time I ran into DMX was in Detroit while he was doing a mini-promo midday concert on a flatbed truck in the park. I went with one of my homies from Detroit, Al Nuke, who also is a rapper. There were about 300 people out there. DMX put on a high energy show. After the show I went into DMX's trailer and told him I was performing at a local comedy club that night and that he should come through. When the 10:30 p.m. show was about to begin that night, I saw DMX and his crew sitting in VIP. I was like *"Damn, dude is real about his."* That night I tore the roof off the club and afterwards I thanked him for coming to my show. Detroit is one of my top three cities to perform in. They just get my comedy. At the end of the night I was bragging to the club owner that I had gotten DMX to come to the club and he said, "Fool, I had to pay that man to be here." Damn, I thought DMX had love for me, but he's got love for the almighty dollar. I can't be mad at him for that. A few years later in Arizona, I saw him once more at the finals of a big talent showcase I was hosting, but he left before I could speak.

Red and Meth went on to have a short lived sitcom on Fox. And DMX, well if you watch the news, you know. It's a shame because he's one of the dopest (no pun intended) in the game.

Dr. Dre *(Rapper, Producer)*

Around the summer of 1996, I was really feeling myself. I had just wrapped up filming *B.A.P.S., How To Be a Player* and Tupac's video *All About You*, when I got a call from another casting director asking if I would be interested in being in a Dr. Dre video. It was for a song called *"Been There Done That."* At this point, Dre had left Death Row, and started his own company, Aftermath Records. People were wondering what he was coming out with and this would be the first single off his new compilation album. It was to be a three-day video shoot. I agreed and being a little full of myself, I told them I wanted $1,500 a day! *"People, we're talking $4,500!"* The average video pays actors $200 per day. I know people who would have done it for free. This was Dr. Dre, a rap legend. But back then, I was on the way to becoming a legend myself (in my own mind). They called back and accepted.

The first day of shooting was at 5 a.m. at a place in the Marina in L.A. I was the first one there because when it comes to getting money, I am always on time. Cars started arriving and people started wandering around, but no Dre. All of a sudden this big Mercedes pulled up and out stepped Dr. Dre. I was a little nervous, but I didn't want to show it. As I approached him and shook his hand, he had a huge smile on his face. I seem to have that effect on a lot of people. He told me he was a fan and was happy I could do the video. I remember thinking I didn't want him to know I had just done a Tupac video for fear of him replacing me. As I said, this was 1996 and he was having beef with Suge Knight and Death Row, and I wanted that $4,500.

I learned what he expected of me in the video. I was to play his chauffeur. The shoot was fun. Dre is easy to work with. He let me do a lot of ad-libbing. I remember one time we were in the limo just riding from one location to another, and I asked him if there were any artists he had a chance to sign that he passed on. To my amazement he said MC Breed (remember the song *"Aint No Future in Yo' Frontin'?"*) Remember, this was years before Eminem and 50 Cent.

The video was a hit even although the album wasn't. MTV Video awards even nominated the video for Best Dance sequence. Remember the *"Ghetto Tango?"*

A few times, Dre invited me to parties at his home on the outskirts of L.A. I shouldn't even say home, this shyt was a palace. One of those kinds of homes you can't see all of the first couple of times. His property sat on so much land; he was talking about playing a real flag football game on one of his "little" pieces of land. I was thinking, is this the same dude from the World Class Wrecking Cru, with the glittery glove, Jheri Curl and leather boots, who later said *"Fuck the Police?"* I thought damn, it's time for me to put on some gloves and boots, and tell the police to lick one of my balls.

Dre asked to sign me to his label, but I turned it down. The deal was $15,000 for five comedy albums. I was making more than $5,000 per show, so this didn't impress me, Dr. Dre or not (remember I was feeling myself). Hell, I had just turned down $225,000 from Sony TV (that's another story). (Please don't slap me. Hell, I probably needed to be slapped.) Dre did call me into the studio to do some skits on the *Chronic 2000* album, but we could never come up with anything. Well truth be told, he changed his mind. Dre is such a perfectionist, sometimes too much. So Dre, can we get that *Detox* album already? I haven't seen much of Dre in the past few years. But I am thankful I got a chance to hang with one of the dopest producers in all of music.

(See photo)

Dru Hill *(Singing group)*

I was on the *Budweiser Super Fest Tour* in the fall of 1997, and our first stop was in Buffalo, New York. I was walking around backstage checking everything out, when I saw Sisqo going over some dance steps with some girls. I stood to the side and watched him. I remember what stood out was his blond hair, the earring in his eyebrow, how short he was, and the fact he had on a matching leather jacket and pants, NO shirt. I had seen him in videos but I'm always taken aback by how small some of these stars are (for the record I'm 6'1").

Then the rest of Dru Hill came out of their dressing rooms. This was during the time they had hot singles like *"Tell Me," "In My Bed"* and *"We're Not Making Love No More."* They were the opening act, followed by Ginuwine, Aaliyah, Mary J. Blige, and Bone Thugs 'N' Harmony. Dru Hill did a very good job opening the show, which is not an easy job. Each member brought something different to the performance, but Sisqo was the stand out in the group. You could just tell he was going to leave that group one day.

All the girls wanted to get backstage to meet Sisqo. I could sense a little jealousy from the other members, especially Nokio. I would find out later that Dru Hill was really his group that he put together. It turns out they were from Baltimore, Maryland, not too far from where I grew up. So they became my homeboys. They said they got their name from a street there called Druid Hill.

A lot of people thought Sisqo was gay. From my experience of being on tour with him for six weeks, I'll tell you that there was never a sign of that. He was chasing and accepting the attention from the ladies way too much. I think his flair is what made people think he was gay. I'll chalk it up to him being an artist. And sometimes artists are different. Hell, I've been wearing a charm bracelet for years, but you can ask a few females if I am gay.

Now late one night in Miami, I did have a painful experience with Sisqo while a part of my body was exposed, that I still feel to this day. Hold up. That didn't sound right, let me explain *quickly*. Dru Hill knew this popular tattoo artist named Rob who owned his own shop. So after the show one night, we all went and got tattoos. I got my first tattoo: "Bianca," my daughter's name around my arm. I'm gonna keep it real, that shyt was so painful, it would be ten years before I would get another one. People say tattoos are addictive. Shyt! Now Nokio was addicted. He was one of the first dudes to really get tatted up. I mean hands, neck, face, you name it. We later went to a strip club called Rolex that night. Hanging with those dudes was so much fun. They had a road manager (I think his name was Keith) that was my dawg. We clicked quickly and had so much fun. Jazz was a bit quiet and a little stand-offish. Woody seemed to be shy, he really didn't speak up much around strangers. But if he got to know you, he was cool. I liked Nokio because I could tell he felt like he was in charge of the group; he and Sisqo had a lot of ideas.

After that tour I wouldn't see them again, and was a bit saddened when I heard they broke up. But I saw it coming. From what I saw, they were never really a group, more like four talented individuals coming together and forming a "group." But when they were hot, they were hot.

Eddie Griffin *(Comic, Actor)*

I had just arrived in Hollywood in 1991, and was willing to perform any and everywhere. I heard about an audition for a talent show, and that "certain people" would be there, so I decided to enter. The usual cast of characters was there, people who thought they could sing, rap, tell jokes, and dance. You meet some of the strangest people at these showcases (you've seen *American Idol* auditions). As people went up to perform, I sat back thinking this was going to be a breeze, there was no way I wouldn't be discovered. Everyone feels this way when they come to Hollywood for the first time. Besides, there was nowhere near as many Black comics working in Hollywood back then as there are now. Hell, there weren't even that many Black comics in the country.

I saw this guy dressed in some sweatpants and karate shoes, with a floppy hat and a jacket tied with a belt on the OUTside of the jacket. I thought, "W*ho the hell is this fool?? Is the Black circus in town or something?*" His name was called, which I didn't hear, and he began to perform comedy. The energy, timing and personality this dude had shook me. I thought if these guys coming straight off the street are this funny, I'm in trouble. He tore down the house; people were falling out of their chairs. I thought to myself this was the funniest amateur I had ever seen! Before I knew it he was done and had disappeared. I wanted to meet him just to see if he was real. I've been in many amateur talent shows and ain't no comic been that funny.

My turn came and I did well enough to get picked for the main talent show, which wound up being some more bull. He didn't perform on it. That night I decided to go to the Comedy Store on Sunset to watch other comics. It was the biggest comedy club in the country at that time. I wasn't a regular there yet; you first had to showcase for the owner, Mitzi, and if she liked you, she'd invite you to come back another time. If you passed approval the second time, you could get booked in her club. I peeped into the main showcase room where all the big time comedians performed: Richard Pryor, Robin Williams, Arsenio Hall, Steve Martin, etc. I watched as they announced the next comedian. Who walked out? Eddie Griffin, the guy I had seen at the audition earlier that day. I thought to myself, *"This nigga ain't no amateur."* I felt much better knowing that the level of comics I would face in these talent showcases weren't going to be on his level. What a relief!

The next time I ran into him was at the Def Jam taping in New York. Anyone who has seen Eddie on Def Jam knows he did his thing. Some White female production coordinator was telling me about this guy named *"Eddie Griffin"* who does this hilarious Michael Jackson impression, and I was like *"Yeah, yeah, OK, what about me?"*

I would see Eddie around comedy clubs as the years went by. His star rose so fast, but he would still perform at the Comedy Store regularly, so we would hear about everything he had coming up directly from him. I wished many times that I was doing some of the things he was doing; I knew it was just a matter of time. I can say he was always a good dude to me. It's funny that in all these years, he and I have never shared the same stage. Eddie is and always will be a true force in comedy.

Eddie Murphy, Johnny Gill, & Sugar Ray Leonard *(Actor/Comic, Singer, Boxer)*

It was July 4, 1996 and a friend of mine from D.C. invited me to Johnny Gill's house for a cookout. And since Johnny is from D.C., I was down. We pulled up to the house in a very nice upscale neighborhood. There was plenty of luxury cars parked along the street in front of his house. We rang the doorbell and a dude with dark shades on and twists in his hair opened it up. We walked in and he directed us to the game room downstairs. I was thinking to myself, "*That dude looks familiar. I know I've seen him somewhere before, but I can't put my finger on it.*"

We entered the game room and I saw Johnny Gill, Sugar Ray Leonard and a few other guys chilling, playing video games. I then realized that the dude at the door who looked familiar was in fact, Eddie Murphy. It turned out he was in the middle of filming *Metro*. I was surprised that he wasn't as tall as I was. But here I was face to face with the man who inspired me to pursue a career in comedy. This was the same man whose albums I snuck and listened to in the basement, and whose house I drove to when I first got to California. It used to be owned by Cher. I stood outside the gate and just looked at it. My boy introduced me, saying "Hey fellas, this is my homeboy Pierre from D.C." Eddie said, "Yeah, that's the BET guy." Now at that time, I was feeling myself, I had just finished filming *B.A.P.S.* and *How to Be a Player*, I had appeared on *Def Comedy Jam* a few times, and had done some other shows. I had done BET *Comicview*, but that was the lowest of my career. So I jokingly said to Eddie (even though he was hot off *The Nutty Professor*), "Yeah, you're the *Best Defense* guy" (that was his third movie after *Trading Places* and *48 Hours*, and it DIED at the box office). I could tell I had hit a sore spot. You could have heard a pin drop. Everyone looked at Eddie, then at me, and then back at Eddie. I thought *"Oh shit,"* but then Eddie chuckled and everybody else chuckled. It was one of those *"Fool this is Eddie Murphy, you low-budget-ass comic"* kind of chuckles. I felt like I was in one of those *Southwest* airlines commercial "you wanna get away?" I kept a cracked smile on my face for like five minutes after that. I never felt that nervous before.

Johnny was really cool. I told him that I was also from D.C. and that I remembered him coming up with Staci Lattisaw (they were the Donnie and Marie of D.C. back in the mid 80's). We laughed and he told me to enjoy his house. There were many pretty women and kids playing and cooking. Everyone wound up being cool with me, and I enjoyed my 4th.

Throughout the years I would see Eddie around at Comedy Clubs. I would say "What's up?" but I always wondered if he remembered that I was the guy who made that futile attempt at a joke that day at Johnny's house.

Eminem *(Rapper, Actor)*

In 1999, Dr. Dre called me into the studio to work on some skits for his new album *The Chronic 2000*. I'm friends with one of his producers, Mel Man, who *loves* to Jone. So when I got into the studio, Mel started me up, wanting me to Jone. I noticed Dre in the booth rapping *They Forgot About Dre*, but he was taking direction from a White guy behind the boards (I thought he was an engineer). He was talking to Dre about how to RAP. How dare this *White* guy tell Dr. Dre how to rap! But I could hear the song, and his voice was on the track...and he sounded kind of nice. He was very precise with every word that he wanted Dre to say and how he wanted Dre to say it. They took a break, and Dre came in to the engineering booth to show me love. Mel jumped right in, saying "Pierre, fuck with him!" pointing at the White guy. I was like "Naw, he's just chilling," plus he looked reserved and I never Jone on someone who looks defenseless. But Mel wanted me to get in that ass so bad. Then the White guy started saying that he was a rapper, and talked about how he had gotten booed at a club in Philadelphia. I was thinking, "*You're White and you were in Philly. They don't play that. The last White rapper out was Vanilla Ice, and Black people still haven't forgiven y'all for that!*" Remember, this was 1999. But I did think he was good, even with just that little bit I heard on that song. They were working on the song *"They Forgot About Dre."* A month later I was at home watching MTV and the video for *"My Name Is"* came on and the rest is history. I went out with Mel Man and bought a copy the first day the album came out. And to think, I met one of the biggest rappers to ever hold a mic, before he blew up!

Emmitt Smith *(Pro football player)*

In October 2001, I was living in Dallas. I was out at a club one night when this young guy approached me and told he was a huge fan. His name was Reggie Swinton; he was a kick returner for the Dallas Cowboys. We struck up a pretty cool conversation and exchanged numbers. He invited me to a game and I told him I'd invite him to one of my shows. A few days later he called and asked if I wanted to come to Emmitt Smith's house for a party. Emmitt was throwing a party for all of the young players on the team, to help them build some team chemistry. Smart move, the team had lost a lot of their star players. I got directions and headed to Emmitt's house, which was in a really nice area. When I pulled up, it looked like a mini mansion. Reggie met me at the door. The inside was beautifully done, it had a beautiful staircase, with a walkway that stretched from one side of the upstairs to the other and overlooked the foyer and living room. The kitchen was huge with food everywhere! Oh, I don't know if you know by now but I keep's it real. If you invite me over for food, I'm eating. There won't be any "I'm too cool to eat" coming from me.

I saw this little girl about six running around with all this energy, just enjoying herself. She looked like a female version of someone I knew well. Then I ran into Emmitt. I found him to be very engaging, with a huge smile, and a little shorter than I expected. When you think of Emmitt with all his toughness, and accomplishments, you think of him to be a big man. I guess heart can't be judged by height and weight. He was cool. He knew who I was and told me to enjoy his home. Then I ran into his wife Pat, a real sweet person. We knew each other from Hollywood when she was trying to break into acting a few years earlier. But many people may know her as Martin Lawrence's first wife. And that's who that little girl looked just like. Think of a female version of Martin, but as a cute little girl.

The party was great. Many well-to-do Black people and few White folks, also some very sexy women. Damn it's good to be a Cowboy! As I left, all I could think was that one day I would have a home as classy and nice as that. Not too big, but just right.

Erykah Badu *(Singer)*

In 1993, I was working at Steve Harvey's comedy club in Dallas. I had just come off of *Def Comedy Jam* but I was far from being a "hood-hold" name. But I was moving in the right direction. Steve was giving me another chance to redeem myself from that shit I'd done at his last club (See the Steve Harvey story). This club was a step up. This was a real comedy club, not a nightclub turned into a comedy club. So I felt more at home.

There was this sexy female club manager there with a strange voice, which made her even sexier. She was around my age or a little younger, which struck me as odd. Most club managers are either men or older women. I flirted with her a few times during my week there. I'm sure she had probably heard it all from all the comics that came through there. She was sweet and played the flirty moments just right. Every time I was in her presence my temperature would rise, and that doesn't happen very often. She had these eyes that were captivating, and a perfect booty—and I'm a booty man. Every show I did there, I would kill, hoping she would notice. One day she told me that I was very funny. That was a big deal; being a manager at that club, she had seen a lot of comics. At the end of the week she called me into her office and I thought it was finally about to be on! I straightened my clothes, cleared my throat, sprayed some breath spray and walked in. But no, she called me in there to sign my paper work and get paid. Damn, so close but so far.

A few years later I was watching BET, and the video for the song *"On and On"* came on. I kept watching the TV thinking I knew the girl singing from somewhere, but I couldn't put my finger on it. A few weeks later I picked up a hip-hop magazine as I was boarding a plane, and as I skimmed through the pages I came upon that face again. I quickly read the article and discovered that she was the young manager who had worked at Steve Harvey's club. Miss Erykah Badu. The next thing I knew, she was the hottest thing in the NeoSoul movement. Her vibe was stranger than I expected, with the afro centric look going on. I always thought she was sexy as hell, but I felt like she was covering up what I knew was behind all that damn cloth. I caught her act in 2005 at a club in Washington, D.C., called Dreams. She put on a great two hour show, and was very in tune with the audience. I decided to go downstairs to handle some business and figured I would return in a little while to talk to her and remind her of meeting me back at Steve's club. But by time I came back upstairs, she was gone.

I haven't seen her in person since that night, but one day I caught her new video, *"Window Seat,"* with her in all of her glory. Finally she showed the world what I knew she was working with. Like most of my boys said, "DAYUUMNN!!!" Oh yeah, the song was good too. There are three men I'm aware of who are lucky enough to have been with her (she has three kids). They say she's dating Jay Electronica. Can you say Lucky Guy #4! I just sit back and think, *"I remember you when..."*

Fabolous *(Rapper)*

I was at a party during All Star weekend in Denver in February 2005. I was being invited to every party that weekend you can think of, I was hitting like four a night. It may sound like fun, but it's really a lot of work. Well there was a hot party everyone was trying to get into and I was invited, so I slid my happy ass up in there. I spotted Fabolous chilling with a few folks, and went over to show him some love. I don't have too big of an ego, if I see someone I'm a fan of, I'll express it. Hey, many celebrities show me genuine love, so I pay it forward. I said what's up to him and asked if I could take a picture, and he kind of gave me that *"You-were-last-year's-news"* look. I thought *"motherfucker, next year someone is going to give YOU that look."* I took the picture and went back to my homeboys. But I didn't have a good feeling about this nicca.

I saw him once more a few years later in Atlanta, in a little club I was performing at. I didn't even speak to him, because he was last year's news. I trip when people get a little shine in this business and then start smelling themselves. One thing NO one can say is that I treated them wrong if they came at me pure and with kindness. I'll tell any young artist, you may not always be as hot as you are now. One day the shoe will be on the other foot and then you'll get a chance to taste the sole of the very shoe you kicked others with. I don't know, maybe I caught him at a bad time. But if I see that dude out again and I say "What's up?" and I get the same reaction, in my next stand up I'll do ten minutes worth of material on his ass.

(See photo)

Flava Flav *(Rapper)*

I was at Roscoe's Chicken N Waffles on Pico Boulevard in L.A. one night in the summer of 2004, and noticed two dudes standing by the cars in the parking lot. I thought to myself, *"Damn that nicca's dark! And is he breaking into my shit???"* As I approached, I noticed it was Flava Flav, and he was hanging with Rodney Allen Ripply (70's actor). I can't front, I got a little excited because this was a member of one of my favorite rap groups of all time. I was thinking "What the hell are you doing out here in LA?" He told me he was working on a new reality show. I thought, *"Good luck with that bullshit."* You gotta remember, this was before the bullshit reality show explosion. I was thinking, who wants to watch his ass?? Can we say *Surreal Life...? Hello!* Well, he shot the show and...need I say more?

I'm a lot more of a fan of his now than ever before. For someone to take that abuse and still walk with his horned crown up high, *and* do it with a smile. He's a better man than me! Because I would have CLOWNED all those women on that show to the point, there wouldn't have been a season two.

Gabrielle Union *(Actress)*

I first met Gabrielle during All Star weekend in Denver in February 2005. That weekend I was guest of a friend of mine, Rodney, who is a promoter in the area. One of my homeboys, Bilal, called and told me he was at a restaurant eating with a few ladies and invited me to meet him there, so you know I was on my way. Bilal is one of those dudes who's always connected with folks but you really don't know what the hell he does for a living. Whenever something hot is happening, he's always there. Great guy though. When we got to the restaurant and walked up to his table, he was in full conversation with a table full of ladies about relationships. And who was the most vocal of the crew at the table? Gabrielle. And yes fellas, she is just as fine in person. I was digging her because there was no uppity air about her. She wasn't trying to act cute or say all the right things. She tried to drag me into the conversation, but I knew me; I was liable to start a riot with my opinionated ass, so I played it cool. But Rodney was sitting over there looking at Gabrielle, eyes damn near popped out of his head and his tongue damn near on the floor, looking as excited as R. Kelly at a Miss Teen USA pageant! So before I got myself embarrassed, I told them we were making some runs and would meet up with them later.

We met up with Bilal, Gabrielle and her crew at a hotel a few hours later and decided to go to a club. The line to get in was super long, but as we approached the door, someone recognized Gabrielle and asked her if she wanted to be escorted to the VIP area. We were like *"Sure!"* Who the hell wants to stand outside? They took us upstairs to the VIP lounge. I saw Charles Barkley talking to some White women (as expected), and Dennis Rodman chilling, surrounded by a group of White people (also as expected). Does this dude know ANY Black people? We sat at a table and the server brought us a bottle. We poured and toasted the evening. Rodney and I chilled and talked to a few chicks. Kenny Smith was the host of the party and came to speak with Gabrielle. Then Gabrielle wanted to dance with me and I took the opportunity to get close to one of the most beautiful actresses in Hollywood. Rodney kept his eye on Gabrielle and me. After dancing, we were finally ready to leave, and the server gave Gabrielle a bill for $800. Three hundred bucks to be in VIP, three hundred bucks for the bottle and two hundred for other drinks! We were all taken aback, damn, that's a lot! I know some of ya'll reading this are thinking that ain't nothing for stars. Shyt, $800 for drinks and a seat is $800 for drinks and a seat, fuck that! I know most people's monthly rent ain't that much! Gabrielle was about to pay it even though she thought it was a bit much. Rodney wasn't going for that bullshit. He told the waiter, "You asked us if we wanted to go to VIP, we didn't ask you. You brought us a bottle we didn't ask for." So after all was said and done, the bill was reduced to $280. VIP area: price-y. A savings of $520: price-less.

A lot of famous dudes were trying to get at Gabrielle, trying to see if she'd come back to their hotel or go for a "night cap." I can't blame them, she is sexy. But she sweetly turned them down. Nelly (the rapper) had invited her to his party across town and she wanted to stop by there. Gabrielle's ride wanted to stay at this party, so I suggested that she, Bilal and the rest of my crew could roll with us in Rodney's truck. When we got to Rodney's old 1995 Ford Explorer, we had too many people to sit comfortably. Gabrielle didn't skip a beat and said, "Hell I'll sit on someone's lap in the backseat." I was impressed with how down to earth she was, not only sitting cramped in the backseat, but getting in a 1995 Ford Explorer during All Star weekend. Most famous people try to floss so hard during that weekend. They wouldn't be caught dead in an old-ass truck.

I remember she had to pee really, really badly, and she wished she had done so at the last party. During the drive over she kept saying how hard it was for her to hold it in. Rodney was speeding through traffic like he was an ambulance driver. We finally got to Nelly's party, at a club way out in the country. The parking lot was packed with around 300 cars, and it was made out of dirt (it was like we were a field). We had to park like 100 hundred yards away from the building. By this time Gabrielle couldn't hold it anymore. She jumped out of the car and was headed around the back of my boy's truck to do her thing. That's my kind of girl, one who keeps it 100% real. Suddenly she spotted a police car ten feet away. She re-buckled her pants and we had to make a mad dash for the club. People were trying to stop her to talk but she had no words for them. When we got to the front door of the club, there was a huge crowd and when they noticed her, people started trying to get her attention. Even the club owner wanted to talk. All she said was "Where's the bathroom?!" and did a Marian Joyner sprint to find it. A few minutes later she came back outside with the biggest smile on her face.

Nelly had a trailer parked outside the club where he was chilling with his crew, so Gabrielle and I went inside of it while our entourage chilled outside. I met Nelly and was taken aback by how small in stature he was. But he's a really nice guy. Rodney and I stayed a few minutes longer at the club and then left Gabrielle and her crew and went to another spot. But all I could think about was how cool and down to earth Gabrielle was. You don't find many women that fine, especially famous women, to be that fun and down to earth. She's going to make a good wife for some man. Gabrielle, holla if you need something.

Ginuwine *(Singer)*

It was the second show on the *Budweiser Super Fest Tour* in August 1997, and I saw Ginuwine, who was hot off his single *"Pony."* He was new on the scene and the girls were crazy about him. I was sitting in the stands watching Ginuwine on stage. After a few minutes he took off his shirt and the girls went crazy! I noticed he had some glitter on his body, but I figured maybe he had hugged someone wearing glitter before he went on stage. Before he sang his hit "*Pony,*" he would take off his jewelry, jump off stage and run into the crowd, and of course it would be mayhem. The next night was the same thing, even the glitter. By the third night I was like hold up, this nicca is wearing glitter! I went backstage to confirm if my suspicion was right and guess what—it was. He was all sparkly!

When I met him, he was cordial and loved to laugh. He seemed to be a really down to earth guy. I found out we grew up in the same area and went to the same school district. But that's where our similarities ended. I would watch as security would bring young girls back to his dressing room for a private "autograph." They would stand outside his door until he gave them that special "autograph" and then take them back to their seats, smiling. I'm not saying something happened in there...sometimes it can take fifteen minutes to write your name. I can't lie, I was kinda of jealous. I had to work to meet girls, and his singing, baby hair having, curled up sideburns, glitter wearing ass had girls brought to him. Hey, being an R&B star ain't bad work if you can get it.

One day we pulled into a town and I was at the hotel check-in counter, checking myself in. I came across a list of names being checked in. This list had all the performers' real names: Dana Haughton (Aaliyah), David Love (Kid Capri), Elgin Lumpkin (?). I thought, *"Who the fuck could Elgin Lumpkin be and why would someone name their child Elgin?"* I looked up and it was Ginuwine. Damn I don't know if he would have had the same effect in the music scene if announcers would have had to say, "Ladies get ready for the sexy sounds of *EEELLLLGin Lumpkin!"* Good move G.

As I got to know Ginuwine, I saw that he was actually cool and not a dickhead like many R&B dudes can be. As the years went by I saw his star rise. We would run into each other many times, sometimes even sharing the stage. We would always talk about the great times we had on that tour. He was and is still a big fan of mine as I am of his. I don't think he gets the respect he deserves. OK, OK, I know he might not be the greatest R&B singer of all time, but you have to respect his body of work. He should be respected due to the fact that he is still making music to this day. Ginuwine is my dawg for life.

Ginuwine-" Hanging at a club in Atlanta"

Halle Berry *(Actress)*

Halle is the one person **EVERYONE** asks me about. Well, I'll give you as much detail as I remember. Back in March 1996, I used to do the warm ups (keep audiences entertained between sets for live shows) for the TV shows *The Fresh Prince of Bel Air* and *In Da House*. One day I was working on the *In Da House* set, up in the bleachers with the audience. If you stand in front of the front row, you can't really see the faces of people in the front row. But I noticed these two attractive women; one had a baseball cap on, and the other was a little heavyset. So as I walked past I commented to the heavyset one, "Girl you like Halle Berry's sister," a weak attempt at humor. The audience laughed. After the taping, I noticed that it *was* Halle Berry in the baseball cap. I didn't notice her until the audience was leaving. As she walked out the studio, I felt like a fool.

A few weeks later Robert Townsend called me to come meet him at the Beverly Hills Hotel, no explanation. Hey, when you're a young comic and Mr. Townsend calls you, you come. I pulled up to the hotel, walked in and was greeted by Charlie, Robert's female assistant that I knew from other encounters with him. She said, "Don't lose your mind and don't trip, but you're about to meet Halle Berry." I thought, *"Oh great...when she sees me, SHE might trip."* I walked in and Robert, Halle and the heavyset woman were sitting in a booth. Yes fellas, Halle's just as fine in person as in the movies. Robert did the proper introductions and we began to talk about me: where I was from, why I got into comedy, what projects I wanted to do, etc. After about fifteen minutes, Robert said thank you for coming. I thought *"Thanks for what motherfucker, getting me out of bed on a Sunday morning to meet Halle Berry?"* So, I left and had no idea what that meeting was for.

A few days later Robert called to tell me I had the part in his new movie *B.A.P.S.,* and I would play the love interest of Halle Berry. Folks, I had never been in a movie before, and now I was about to star with one of the most sought-after actresses in Hollywood. Talk about life changing in a split second! I went home and told my wife to pack her bags with her prettiest outfits, a beautiful island was calling. She asked, "What beautiful island are we going to?" I said, "We? Ain't no we, YOU getting the hell up outta here." Naw, I didn't say that...(laugh)

While rehearsing Robert would take the four of us (Natalie Deselle, AJ Johnson, Halle and I) out places so that we could build up better chemistry. I found out that Halle had a big influence on who would play her boyfriend. She chose me out of all the actors she met. I thought, "*Well, this might lead to something outside filming.*" (Who wouldn't want to be her boyfriend even if you're married?) So I never brought up the fact I was married, besides it wasn't asked. I had the Army policy back then: Don't Ask, Don't Tell. And she seemed to really be digging me, or maybe it was just in my head. But either way I was going to roll with it, just for the sake of the chemistry of the film. She wanted to come and see me perform stand up, and hang out so I gave her my cell phone number. This was during the time she was splitting up with David Justice.

One day I had to go to rehearsal and didn't have a babysitter for my six month old daughter, so I had to bring her to rehearsal. Halle saw my baby and asked if I was married, and when I said yes it seemed like all the chemistry I felt we had left her body. I look at my daughter today and think *"Girl, do you know who your stepmother could have been?"*...(laugh). I can respect what Halle was going through though. She's too classy to want to get involved with a married man. Hell, she's been cheated on and she knows how that feels. In hindsight, I was lucky to have such a great wife.

I had a great time filming. I learned filmmaking ain't no joke. There's no time for playing around, you have too much money invested. Now, let me tell you about the most asked about scene: the kiss. The scene was supposed to start with us dancing, cut to the old man in the hospital, then cut back to us dancing, cut to him dying, then cut back to us kissing and dancing. Well we were running out of time filming and I overheard that we were going to skip the kissing part. I thought "*Shit, I'm a brother from D.C. We'll have no skipping shit, especially kissing Halle Berry. We can skip all the rest of my scenes in this movie but I'll be damned if we're skipping that.*" So when we started dancing, I just went for it and kissed her. I thought Halle might pull back and say, "Oh no, we're skipping that part," but being that she's a great actress (she really is) she went with the moment. And the rest is lip-locking history. We only did one take of that kiss and you got to see it.

Do you remember the scene where she was crying when she saw me? Well she had to do that take like five times. I was blown away by how she could cry on cue. Each time Robert would say "cut," they would dry her eyes and after they said "action," her eyes would well up with water. Talk about talent.

I only saw her a few more times after that and she would always show love. She has no idea what that kiss did for my player status. Every man and some women ask about that kiss. Thanks, Halle, you're a sweetie.

P.S…I heard she just recently broke up with her boyfriend. I might finally have a chance!

Heavy D *(Rapper)*

Around 1996, I first met Heavy at a boxing gym in L.A. He was the president of Uptown Records at the time and was working out to stay in shape. I walked into the gym and noticed this big 250-plus pound brother, wrapping his hands to get ready to box. As I got closer, I was shocked to see that it was Heavy. He's not a guy I would expect to see at a boxing gym. We hit it off right away. He is everything most people think he is, fun, lovable, and likes to joke around. I asked him if wanted to get in the ring and much to my surprise he said yes. It was something we would do a few times. Heavy has some skills. He was in there with a cat from D.C. And D.C. guys are usually good with their hands. That's all we did as kids, everyone wanted to be Sugar Ray Leonard. I took it easy on him, but Heavy hung in there and stood his ground. We talked about a movie that I wrote that I was trying to get made, and he seemed genuinely interested in being in it. He had me drop off a script to the Four Seasons Hotel he was living at. I never made the movie, but Heavy was and is a cool dude. Now I see why so many people love him. I would run into him around Hollywood and we would always joke about taking it back into the ring. I got nothing but love for ya' Heavy.

(See photo)

Hill Harper *(Actor, Author)*

I first met Hill at the Acapulco Black Film Festival in 2000. I was screening *For Da Love of Money.* I saw him walking around. I knew of him, hell, he was my Hollywood competition. But we never said anything more than pleasantries to each other. But on the flight back from Mexico I ended up sitting next to him. I remember not drinking *any* of the water while I was in Mexico. I was told that would be a wrong move. I had been there twice before and had seen friends lose it (get the runs), so I stayed away from it. Well the flight attendant asked if I wanted something to drink, so I said "Sure, Coke, NO ice." Well when I got my Coke, I noticed it had two ice cubes in it. What's two little ice cubes, right? I started drinking and talking to Hill. I never realized what a deep and highly educated brother he was. He went to Harvard Law School with Obama! Well hell, I did six months at a community college, and here we are sitting on the same plane. He's a good, positive brother. I have a lot of respect for him.

The next thing I knew my stomach started to hurt and we still had about four hours left on the flight! As each minute passed, the pain became more and more unbearable. All I know is I ended up leaning on his shoulder. I was bent over, damn near in his seat for the rest of the flight. By the way things looked, if someone had taken a photo of that moment, it would have made the front cover of the National Enquirer and I would have had a lot of explaining to do to my female fans. But Hill was a good sport about it. That was the first time I ever got food poisoning. I don't wish that on my worst enemy.

I haven't seen him since then, but I did buy his book, *Letters to a Young Brother*. Which was a great read. I watched as his career flourished, and as he went on the campaign trail with President Obama and represented young black men so well with the media. So Hill, thanks for being a cool brother. Much love.

Ice Cube *(Rapper, Actor)*

I never really "met" Cube. I was supposed to. I had an audition for the movie *Next Friday*, and I went in and killed it. My agent got a call a few days later saying the director, Steve Carr, really liked my audition (they had taped it). He and the producers wanted to see me in person. A lot of times your first audition is for just the casting director, and sometimes they put you on video tape. The director watches the tapes and chooses who he or she wants to see in person.

First let me say, I had heard that Mike Epps had gotten that part already a month earlier, so I wasn't too keen on reading a script and memorizing lines for a role that was already booked. I heard Cube really liked Mike, but the director wanted to see other people. So I went in there and did my thing. Well at the call back, the director and producers were running late. I was told they couldn't get one of the producers into the room to watch the few finalists. After awhile I had to use the bathroom, and went walking around looking for one. I ran into a producer friend of mine who had worked on *For Da Love of Money* so I stopped to talk to him. Right over his shoulder, about ten feet away, I could see Cube talking to some people. It looked like they were trying to get him into the room to watch us. He caught me looking at him and looked away. At that point, I understood. It's a shame because I've always been a fan of Cube's film and music career, and would have loved to have been in one of his films. I will say he made a great choice with Mike, but I know I would have hit it out the park.

Ice-T *(Rapper, Actor)*

I first met Ice-T when we were guests on a late night talk show, *Vibe,* around 1997. We both clowned about people thinking light-skinned brothers were out. This brother was so damn cool; just a real shit talking motherfucker. He's a funny brother. The next time I ran into Ice was in the summer of 1999 on the *Warp Tour* in Montreal. The *Warp Tour* is a music tour that caters to the X-Games crowd, so I was wondering what the hell he was doing on it. But if you know Ice, you know he don't give a fuck, he walks to his own beat. If he felt like it, he would play at a police academy graduation. Ice was looking out the window of his trailer, just clowning people walking by. He saw me and invited me in. I met his boys, and they were cool as hell. I joined him at the window, because you know I like to clown! They called him to the stage to perform, and I went onstage with him and his crew. We had a ball that day. He invited me to his office in Hollywood when I got back, and you know me. When I got back I went up there to see what they were doing. He was trying to push some artist on his label. I hung for a minute and was off. Ice-T is a brother you would want to hang with. I never ran into him again, but have a feeling I will one day soon.

A quick side story: I met Ice T's ex-wife, Darlene, at a club in Pomona years before I met Ice and she asked me to dance. Anyone who has seen her knows she's sexy as hell (look at the Power album). We were dancing and laughing, and she seemed to be digging me. I was thinking I should go for it, but all I could think of was Ice coming to my house with fifty gang members, wanting to have a little talk with me. So I fell back, gave her a hug and went home. Fear had never kept me from a woman, but it sure did that night.

Jamie Foxx *(Comic, Actor, Singer)*

As soon as I reached L.A. in September 1990, I told my roommates I was going to a comedy club. They started talking about this guy named Jamie Foxx who they had seen at the comedy clubs. They said that he was funny as hell, and that he did this impression of this ugly girl that was outrageous. My first thought was, *"what nicca is named Jamie?"* I thought he was Mexican working at Black comedy clubs.

One day my roommates escorted me to the *Comedy Act Theatre* in the hood. I was trying to work my way into that club. We were sitting in the audience when I heard Jamie was next and I thought to myself, *"Ok, this dude better be funny. My roommates have been on his jock a little too hard."* I told myself he couldn't be that funny. As a young comic, you don't want to think another comic is funnier than you.

The emcee (Joe Torry) announced him, and Jamie came on. I was shocked at how he looked; not that he didn't look right, but I had formed another opinion in my mind. He started off funny. My roommates tapped me on the shoulder (it was like the scene out of *Coming to America* when the three barbers are at the youth center watching Sexual Chocolate). I took in the scene around me. Jamie's whole aura exuded confidence as he went from physical comedy to voices to impressions. My cocky demeanor was getting chipped away. The more the crowd was falling out with laughter, the more I was thinking, *"Damn, I got some work to do in this town to set myself apart."* Jamie then went into doing the character that would become

"Wanda" and the crowd was in tears. I can't lie, he had me laughing. He made me a believer.

It's very powerful when an artist lives up to the hype, and he did that night. I would run into him from time to time. I even went to a few of his *"parties."* Let's just say, when the lights go down, it's on. You fill in the blank. But he and I never really hit it off. I'm more friends with some of his close friends, especially his boy Johnny Mac (the most ignorant fool I've ever met). I'm cool with that. Everyone ain't supposed to mesh.

He has proven many people wrong and he's on top of his game now. I was happy when he won an Oscar. He made a lot of comics step up their game when it comes to acting, and not just being funny. I would say he's the most talented comic in the game. *He's the only comic I wouldn't want to follow.* I think I'm funny as hell but he has too many things he can pull out, from singing, playing the piano, to impressions. Jamie is the truth.

Jamie Foxx- at one of his big summer parties

John Witherspoon *(Comic, Actor)*

John was doing *Master P's Comedy All Stars Show* in 1999 at the *Universal Amphitheatre* and I decided to go and check him out. I've been a fan of his ever since *Hollywood Shuffle*. I found myself backstage and I spotted John sitting in his dressing room, and he invited me in. As soon as we saw each other we started clowning like we had known each other forever. I was surprised, as I usually am when famous people know me. He loves to make fun of everything: people, the venue, himself, you name it. I wished him good luck and went to mingle with the rest of the start backstage. John had a great show. Later on that night, he spotted me again backstage and asked me if I could write some material for him. I was honored. He gave me his address and phone number and asked me to come by. A few days later when I was going to call him, I realized I had lost the number and address. I even drove around the neighborhood he said he lived in. Someone had told me what kind of car he had, and I was hoping to spot it. But I didn't.

I saw him again three years later at the Improv in Dallas. I was living there at the time and went to catch him. As soon as I got to the green room (dressing room) he started in on me, asking how I had been, what I had been up to, and why I was living in Dallas. He asked if I wanted to go up on stage, but I politely turned him down. This was his moment, his crowd. I just came to watch him. He did a great job. What I admired about him was that for him to be in his mid 60's, he was still out putting work in at a high level. I just sat back and thought how cool it would be to be sixty and still having all ages laughing. We would share the stage many times after that and I will always look up to him with admiration.

John Witherspoon- In his dressing room at
Master P's Comedy All Stars in LA

Kanye West *(Rapper, Producer)*

I got called in 2004 by Chris Robinson, a well-respected director and friend of mine, to do a cameo in a video for a song called *"Selfish"* by Slum Village, a group that I was a fan of. I went down to the set and saw Chris. We chopped it up for a minute. Then I saw Kanye walking around with a backpack on. I had seen him on TV a few times, but at that time he was nowhere near the star he is today. We spoke and he seemed pretty normal and cool, but I could tell there was something different about him because he reminded me of myself. He would just sit back and watch what others were doing. I could tell he was taking mental notes of everything that was going on. That's what visionaries do!

The guy who really struck me on the set that day was the "new' member of Slum Village. This brother was extra hyper, just jumping around the set. As soon as they would say action, dude was all in the video, all over the place, just seeming to be happy to be in his first video. That "new" guy turned out to be John Legend.

They wanted me to do a part in the video if this one guy didn't show up. But right at the last minute, he showed up. It was that damn Farnsworth Bentley, P. Diddy's man-servant. I didn't get to shoot any other parts in the video because they were taking too long and I had to leave. Yes, I usually get paid for videos, so no money, no stay too long. I did meet rapper Special Ed (one of my favorites) on the set. He was there with his son. We had a nice talk. He's a good dude.

The next time I saw Kanye was a few years later at the Comedy Store. He was a star by then. He was standing alone in the back and I spoke to him. We talked for a brief moment and he was really down to earth. It made me feel good that he remembered me. Funny thing is, people have judged him to be many things, some warranted, others not. He would go on to let his behavior rule him, and let his mouth write a check that he *could* cash. He is a tortured artist in the truest sense, but I understand him fully. He's just a little misunderstood. He is one of my favorite entertainers. I think what he does should be applauded more than scrutinized. Someone like Kanye only comes around once in a generation.

Katt Williams *(Comic, Actor)*

I first met Katt at a club in LA that he hosted. He hired me to headline the show. All I remember was that the club was full of ghetto ass folks. I saw gang bangers, weave, gold teeth, rusty knuckles, saggin' pants—and that was just security! Those are my kind of folks. I grew up performing for those crowds. Katt had a little dressing room for the comics out to the side of the stage. We were all in there getting ourselves ready for the show when Katt walked in. I had seen Katt around the comedy circuit many times, but never really got the chance to kick it with him. I always thought he was funny. A few things struck me about Katt when I saw him that night: how short he was, his outfit (this nicca looked like a Western version of Prince), that he had a few girls working for him (unknown comics usually don't have assistants) and he had what appeared to be no top teeth. But I didn't care. I was there to get this money, not to be his dentist.

It was show time, and Katt went out on stage, grabbed the mic, and from that moment on he had that crowd eating out of his hands. When Katt hosts a show, it makes it hard for the performers to maintain the level of the show. I can say is that there was just something about him. I can't say I thought he would become a star of the magnitude that he later became, but there was something definitely different about him and I didn't know if America was ready for Katt.

I feel bad when I hear some of the news reports about his behavior, from allegedly breaking in people's houses, to going to jail. Because the Katt Williams I know is actually a caring, giving guy.

Kid Capri *(DJ)*

I first met Kid in October 1992, when I performed on *Def Comedy Jam.* We didn't really talk at that time, but I really got to know him later when we were on the *Budweiser Super Fest Tour* in 1997. That tour featured Dru Hill, Ginuwine, Mary J. Blige, Aaliyah, and Bone Thugs 'N' Harmony. I was the emcee and opening act for the tour. The promoter wanted me to ride with the stage crew from city to city. That would have meant I'd have to wait around after the show for them to break down the stage and load it up, then ride to the next city in a truck, get there before hotel check in and sleep in the truck until the hotel room was ready, *oh hell naw!* I was telling Kid this and he said I could ride on his tour bus with his crew. This would be the most fun I have ever had on tour. Six guys on a tour bus together, roaming the country. Need I say more?

Well, I will. First of all, his crew had toured together before so they were like a unit already, but they took me in like I was a brother. Kid is really a fun guy. He has a hip-hop ego. Not in a bad way but he truly wants people to recognize his legendary status. He has a real competitive spirit which you have to have in the cutthroat world of hip-hop. We'd play all kinds of games. One game we played was Area Code. Since he toured so much, all you had to do was name any area code and he knew the city. After years of traveling, I now play this game with my friends. Then some of us played "Who Can Get the Most Girl's Numbers." True, I hadn't been on tour before, but I am blessed with spitting game. After the tour was over and we announced the winner of that game, it was…me! I'm not proud of this but when you're young or young-minded, you do certain things.

These days I don't really go to many after parties. I'm usually back in my room sleep, ready to catch the first flight out.

Kid had a video game system in his bedroom on the bus, where everyone play NBA Live (this was back when you could only play with two players on each team, and the Chicago Bulls had everyone but Michael Jordan on their team). The guys would be back there screaming and laughing. I'm not a video game player; I'd rather read a book or write one (wink). Weeks of me hearing them back there hollering and screaming went by and I wondered what the big deal was with playing video games. One day I was on the bus by myself and decided to go back there and play around with the game and got instantly hooked. My ass was back there all the time for the rest of the tour. After the tour, since I didn't have a video game system, I lost the desire to play one. I haven't touched a video game since. I have a lot of homeboys who play them. I might not play, but I understand their excitement for the games.

Riding with Kid on that tour was better than riding with the other acts because he always had to DJ an after party. So after the concert we would pull the tour bus up to the local club and it was on! You think people like to check out limos? Chicks want to see the inside of tour busses. Do I need to say any more? (I'll save that for my next book).

We bonded so well on that tour, we were like brothers. We had each other's backs. If something went down you had to deal with all of us. Over the years, I would see the fellas separately on different tours or concerts, but none of them was like the tour in 1997. I ran into Kid in Cancun in May 1999. He was hanging with Rapper and DJ Biz Markie. Now that's a dude who can really Jone (just look at him, why wouldn't he?). Biz ain't to be messed with if you ain't prepared. We just chilled outside a café that day, talking about everyone who passed by.

I'll always have love for you Kid, holla at yo boy!

(See photo)

Kid 'n Play *(Rappers, Actors)*

I've never met them together, but I did once audition for their movie *Class Act* (which was anything but…).

I first ran into Kid (the light-skinned one) at the Comedy Store in Hollywood in 1999. I now know he was checking out the comedy scene because he would be entering the ranks of being a stand-up comic. When we met we hit it off instantly; and when I say instantly, I mean *instantly.* We started Jonin' right from the word go. What I like about him is that he doesn't take himself too seriously. And I was impressed with his comebacks and Jonin' ability (the boy is good). I had a totally different image of him. To be honest, I thought he would be *corny*. At this time in his career his last few movies were, let's say, a bit cheesy. And their last album wasn't really what folks were listening to (for the record I did like some of their earlier stuff). But his realness was impressive that night. That night all we did was talk about folks and each other. As the night ended we exchanged numbers and told each other we would stay in touch. Which we celebrities always say, but never do.

I never called him but I would start hearing that he was doing stand-up at different clubs around the country (mostly White and Mexican clubs) and I heard he was actually decent. One night I was watching TV and flipping the channels and came across him doing comedy, so I had to sit back and take it in. He did well, and his material was good. Not on the level of the big boys, but to come from being a rapper to being a stand-up comedian, he did a very good job.

The next time I ran into him in person was at Tommy Davidson's house for a Thanksgiving dinner in 2006, and again as soon as we saw each other, we started in on each other. I love seeing him because he's always ready to laugh. I'm telling you folks, he's not that corny dude from the *House Party* movies.

I was surprised to learn that he wrote the theme music to one of my favorite shows, HBO's *Real Time with Bill Maher*. Throughout the years I've watched as he moved up in the comedy ranks to become a headliner in many comedy clubs. Now we frequently run into each other at the airport. If you get a chance, go out and catch one of his shows.

Now I met Play (the dark-skinned one…) in 2005 in Houston, backstage at the Essence Festival. We both were working the show. Our job was to take the mic to audience members who were answering questions when the host asked questions. He had one side of the arena and I had the other. I was pleasantly surprised to see how humble and down to earth he was. Sitting backstage, I got the chance to kick it with him. We talked about his past movies, living in North Carolina and church. He told me he was a born-again Christian, and talked about the production company he founded. He also said he was teaching at a college in North Carolina.

I remember once, I was on stage at Dangerfield's comedy club in New York City in the mid 90's and I saw Shari Headley (from *Coming to America*) in the audience, and I said to her from the stage, "Are you the one that's married to Play from Kid 'n Play?" And she said, "That's old news." I was like damn, she just fronted dude out like that in front of all these folks. I had a little crush on her then, but after that I was like, that ain't cool. But hey, she was young and I don't know what he did to her. When I met him he was cool, but then again, I wasn't sleeping with him either.

Say what you want about Kid 'n Play, but they put their put their everlasting stamp on hip-hop culture. When you see that kick dance, you know who it belongs to. *(See photo)*

Leon *(Actor)*

Leon saved my life once. I'll get to that in a minute.

I met Leon when I was touring in a play. One of those *"Momma Someone Burned My Cornbread, Girl You Ain't Gots No Man, Where's My Baby Daddy?"* plays around 2003 called *Something She Can Feel*. I was brought on for a little star power (emphasis on *little*), and Leon and I were the top names. He came to our rehearsal with a little bit of an air about himself and people noticed it. So you know me. I didn't give a fuck about this clown. I knew who he was and what he had done, but as far as I was concerned all of us there were equal as far as talent went. We all were bringing something special to that project.

Now I did dig his style of clothing (kind of retro) and when I saw him with something on that was cool, I went out and bought it (hey, I'm keeping it real). His attitude only slightly changed during the weeks of rehearsals. My road manager, another actor and I would go hang out at the mall, and he would go out with his personal chef (yes, he had a chef touring with him). Whenever the girls would recognize me, I'd be taking pictures and signing autographs; then when he came around, they'd leave me in a hot second and scream for him. I can't be mad; big bank takes little bank.

Our dressing rooms were next to each other throughout the tour. I would watch how he would interact with people who came backstage to wish him luck. Very Hollywood-ish to me, but hey, he's been around a lot longer than I have. After the show we would do a curtain call and run to the front of the auditorium to take pictures and sign autographs. He would wait awhile to make his entrance after all the other lead actors came out. In all fairness, a lot of women were waiting for him. He would come out and hide between the wall and cloth backdrop, and peep his head out to get screams. I thought, *"What a clown. This dude is real Hollywood."* He would only take Polaroid pictures, from which he made $5 per photo. I heard he'd make up to $500 a show that way. Not bad for extra change. But he wouldn't do autographs. I thought that was shitty but in fairness, by the time he got done taking pictures, there wasn't much time left to sign autographs. But damn, not one? I think that because he saw how friendly I was with the fans, hugging them, taking free pictures and signing autographs that he started being a little more open as the days went by. I know this as a fact because he stopped running behind the backdrop, and instead came out and jumped on a table and would start to sing *"I know you wanna leave me..."* (From the song *"Ain't Too Proud to Beg." Leon was in the Temptations* movie) and the women would go wild and sing along. He became more open with everyone as time went on, and wasn't a bad guy after all. Every time he would enter the stage for the first time during the play, there would be a minute long scream and he loved every second of it. I know I would have. As an actor, I thought he was OK. I've seen better, but he does have charisma. Many people don't have that.

Now to the part about him saving my life. Whenever I go to a city, I like to explore the city. We were in Chicago, and I met this dude at the play and told him I wanted to out to a club. It was a Tuesday night, and he took me to a club called Glo, a cool spot, but more of a place where Jay-Z, Paris Hilton or Diddy would party. After that night I told him I wanted to go where my 'niccas' would hang out. He said he had just the spot, but it was really jumping on Sundays. I was cool with that. We had two shows on Sunday, but I would be good to go out after that. All week, Leon was asking all of the cast mates to come out and see his band play at this little spot on Sunday after the last show. By that time he was cool with me. So I decided to go watch him and his band that night instead of going to the club. While out watching Leon's band, I didn't realize how tired I was. I slumped in the couch and had damn near fell asleep when I got a call from the dude about coming to get me to take me to the club. I told him I was too tired, and had to pass on the offer. The next morning, I woke up to the tragic news of the deaths that occurred that previous night at club *E2*, the club the dude was planning to take me to. If it wasn't for Leon getting me to come to his show, I would have been at that club. Thanks Leon. God bless the souls that died that day.

I would run into Leon again in May 2010, while starring in the same stage play, *Loving Him is Killing Me.* His personality is still the same, but now that I know him, I know it's just how he is. He's an artist and lives that lifestyle, and many people just don't understand. Overall, he's a good guy.

Leslie Nielsen *(Actor)*

I got a call from my manager one day telling me he had the inside track on a film with Leslie Nielsen (from the *Naked Gun* movies), but they were considering Marlon Wayans for the role of his sidekick. I thought, *"Well, there goes another part I won't be getting."* I went in to meet the producers and they liked me. Well, kind of. They didn't see the crazy guy in me that they wanted in the movie. Sometimes producers will meet you and expect you to be that character when you walk in the door. Not with you studying lines or the script, but they want you to just come in acting a straight nut. My manager and lawyer talked them into giving me the part.

I was off to Munich, Germany, to start filming in June 1999. The producers were German and Canadian and really cool. We stayed in a beautiful five-star hotel in the middle of town, and they gave me a lot of spending money. The first night, the producers took a few of the actors to a very exclusive restaurant. This is where I first met Leslie. The people in Europe are crazy for this dude. They like silly, over-the-top comedies. He is the second-coming of Jerry Lewis to them. He was surprisingly tall and had some big ass hands. I did my homework on him before I met him and found out he started off as a serious actor, until he did the movie *Airplane*. He was in his mid-seventies, and he brought along his gorgeous wife who was in her forties. Damn, life is good when you're famous.

I would be there for six weeks, and I found out I was going to only work five days! I had all day to just walk around. I walked and walked and walked. I would put on my headphones and walk around

Germany at 1 a.m. The jet lag was killing me and I couldn't sleep. I didn't know anyone there and my German was a little rusty, so communication was difficult. It was one of the loneliest times of my life. I would sit in my hotel room for hours watching TV, but my only choices were MTV Europe and BBC News. Think of it, six loooong weeks. A good thing about being in Germany was that I got a chance to go see my mother (she lived five hours away). I caught the train and went and spent some down time with her. One time during filming, my mother came down to the set and I introduced her to Leslie, who she was a big fan of.

I never felt a connection with Leslie during the entire filming. I remember a point when we moved our production to Montreal, Canada, and I had more scenes. Whenever I tried to put some "urban" flair into the scene, he would tell me he didn't like way I was delivering the lines. I once asked Leslie if he had ever heard of Martin Lawrence, Eddie Murphy or Chris Tucker. He'd only heard of Eddie. I knew I was in trouble. One particular day we had a lot of extras on the set, and most were my age. During a break I struck up a conversation with them, and a lot of them recognized me and said how much they liked my past work. They were wondering why I wasn't as funny in this movie. Do you know how much that hurts for comedian to hear? I went to the director and we devised a plan. In the first take, I'd do it my way and then if and when Leslie complained (see, he was also a producer on the film), we would then do it his way. But at least we'd make it so that when it came time to edit the movie, the director would have my first take on film. Man, that was the most nervous I'd ever been on a set.

I got through the movie the best way I could. I heard the movie is out there somewhere, but I refuse to watch it because that's not me. Thanks, Leslie.

(See photo)

Ludacris *(Rapper, Actor)*

The first time I met Luda was at the radio station, WGCI, in Chicago. I was coming into the studio and he was coming out with his crew. He was surrounded by a group of big ass dudes, and I thought, *"Who's this little dude in the middle?"* Then I realized, *"Oh snap, that's Ludacris!"*

The next time I saw him was at a hotel in Arizona during Superbowl weekend of 2008. I was invited there to do some radio sponsored interviews along with a lot of other celebrities. This took place at the outdoor pool of the hotel, and gave fans an opportunity to mingle with us celebrities. I was sitting on a lounge chair at the pool doing an interview, when Ludacris came and sat down next to me to join in. I was excited because I am a huge fan of his. I think he is one of the most underrated lyricists in the game. I introduced myself. He gave me a quick *"What's up?"* as if to say *"yeah, I know you but what are you doing in my section?"* So just to make sure I didn't read it wrong, I decided to strike up conversation. I thought, *"I know this nigga ain't just give me the semi-brush off?"* I spoke again and got another short answer. I thought *"Pierre, be cool and try once more before you clown this nigga."* Luda barely squeezed out a few more words. Now in all fairness, he was being bombarded by interviewers, but I only spoke to him between interviews, and we were sitting damn near hip to hip. I wasn't feeling his vibe, so when I got done, I got up and walked away. I did get along with his manager, Chaka Zulu, though. He was pretty cool. As far as Luda, I'll chalk up our first meeting to bad timing. He's still one my favorite lyricists of all time.

Magic Johnson *(Basketball player)*

It was 1997 and things were going well with my career. I was invited to participate in the annual *A Midsummer's Magic Celebrity Basketball Game* for the first time of many to come. At this game, all the young stars get together and play basketball in front of about 15,000 fans at the Forum in L.A. After that game, then the NBA All Stars play. My favorite part is all the cool stuff you get for participating: new shoes, a uniform with your name on it, electronics, etc. And yes, I was happy to get this stuff. I'll let you in on a little secret. Stars still want FREE shyt, no matter how much money they make. In an instant they could always go back to having nothing.

I went out on the court for the pre-game warm-up. I enjoyed messing with the fans, signing autographs, and taking pictures. I never took the game that seriously, but some of the guys did; at times way too seriously. I felt like we were there for the fans, not to see who was going to win the game. Not that I'm not competitive; when it comes to money, I am. But hell, if your team won, you didn't get anything. While I was shooting around I saw Magic. The first thing that's noticeable about him is his smile (have you ever seen him NOT smiling?). He had people hugging him, wanting to take pictures with him and I thought, *"don't they know this dude's got HIV?"* (This was my ignorance at the time). But people didn't seem to care about that. He came over to where I was shooting and I introduced myself. It's funny, as soon as you meet him and he starts talking to you, he's so disarming that you forget about his disease.

A few weeks later his company, MJM, was interested in doing business with me, so I had a meeting with one of his staff members about managing me. He wanted me to come on board with his company, and offered me a $100,000 holding deal. But the manager I was with at the time begged me not to leave him. My sense of loyalty kicked in and I stayed with him, a move I would regret a few years later.

I would always see Magic out, be it at a Tyson fight, the Essence Festival, you name it. He would always speak, and call me by name. The first few times I was surprised he knew my name. After all, this was *Magic Johnson*, one of the greatest basketball players of all times, someone I grew up watching…and he knows my name!

One thing I admire about him is not what he has done on the court, but what he has done off the court, like the businesses he has. Let's be real, we all know he didn't go to business school and graduate with an MBA. But for him to have amassed the kind of fortune he has off the court, you gotta respect his hustle. I also admire the way he has handled being HIV positive. He lives his life out in the public (he's not hiding at home) which is great hope for those who may be dealing with the same illness. But it can also give young people the false impression that life will be normal, and even good if they get HIV. People have to realize, Magic has the funds to stay in the level of good health that he does. The vast majority of people in this world can't afford what he can and mostly likely won't live the quality of life he lives. It's a false reality. But he's a beacon of hope that living a long, successful life with HIV is possible, and maybe in the near future all people who become HIV positive can also.

Magic's smile lights up a room and makes everyone around him calm down. I enjoy being in his company.

(See photo)

Malik Yoba *(Actor)*

We had to do a quick rehearsal of the play I was in, *Something She Can Feel,* one day mid-tour because Leon had to fly to Hollywood for business. Malik came in and replaced him for that night's performance. Now I wasn't familiar with him, except from the TV show *New York Undercover.* But I did respect him. I knew he had done some plays previously.

The entire cast was in a conference room in the hotel starting our rehearsal. A couple of the cast members and I were laughing and joking around about some bullshyt. All of a sudden Malik stopped and got in our ass about playing around and not paying attention. The room went silent. I looked at my boy and looked at Malik and apologized. Because he was right. He had a lot of lines to learn in a short period of time and I (we) needed to respect that. If I'm wrong, I have no problem with admitting it.

He went on to do a great job in the play. I have mad respect for him coming in and learning his part in one day. It took me two weeks to learn half the shyt he had to learn. I also give Malik props for standing up for what needed to be said.

(See photo)

May May Ali - at the Comedy Store in Hollywood. "Alot of people don't know she does stand up comedy"

Chris Tucker- hanging at a comedy club in North Holly-wood. "Think of how funny a movie would be with Chris and I."

Me, the Biz and Kid Capri in Cancun. "Biz for the sake of humanity, button yo shirt!"

RIP Vernon Forrest: we used to work out in the same boxing gym. He was a good dude.

One of the coolest cats, Cedric the Entertainer- at AllStar weekend in Denver

Fabolous-AllStar weekend in Denver

Terrence Howard: chilling backstage at the Essence Music Festival. Bringing light skin back!

Paul Mooney: chilling backstage with one of my favorite comics. Paul is always so dramatic.

Timbaland: chilling in Cancun. Since the day I met him on tour, when we see each other we just start clownin'.

Heavy D- after working out at the boxing gym in LA

Hanging with two of my favorite actresses-- Yvette Wilson and Kim Whitley

Magic Johnson: at the after party for the Tyson/Lewis fight in Memphis

Malik Yoba: backstage at the play *Something She Can Feel*

Master P: backstage in LA for the taping of the *Comedy All Stars*

Monique: Showing love after taping her show

Leon & Mystikal: backstage at the play *Something She Can Feel.*

Dr. Dre, Fredro Starr, my boy Ben "Yang" Baller, T-Rexx and the crew- at Dre's house for Super Bowl XXX in 1996

On my first trip to LA at Venice Beach: you can tell brothers who are from the DC area; they always pose like this. And "What's up with my hair!?"

Hanging with Kid, Alex Thomas and my boy Gary at the *Players Club* premiere

Ricky Bell: One of the coolest members of New Edition

At the Dallas Improv with Tommy and the coolest club manager Chris

Aaliyah- Showing love at Spike Lee's *He Got Game* premiere. She was one of the sweetest people I've ever known.

Martin Lawrence *(Comic, Actor)*

It was April 1985 and I was going to try stand up comedy officially for the first time. I had signed up earlier that day for amateur night at a local club in D.C. I came back at 9 p.m. for show time. As I entered the club, I saw about thirty comics. They were mostly older White men, with a few White women and five Black comics. As I was sizing up all the comedians I noticed one young brother sitting in the corner. I approached him and introduced myself to him. He said his name was Martin (Lawrence). I can't say we clicked; but as I got to know Martin through the years, I learned that he doesn't really trust many people. I asked how long he had been doing comedy and he said for about a year. I was too naïve at the moment to feel like he was competition, I was just happy to see another person my age in the club. What made Martin succeed was also the thing I don't dig about him and that's his extreme competiveness. Hey, I'm competitive too but not to the point where I gotta have it all. Back then he didn't befriend his direct competition. So to say we hit it off then would be an untrue statement.

I remember the first time we ever got paid for a gig. We performed at a fitness center in the dining area (hey, when you're first starting off you'll perform anywhere). The promoter gave me $15 and gave Martin $50. I was on my way to the Big Time. In 1987, Martin got picked to do *Star Search*. This was a very big deal because this was national exposure. You gotta remember, besides *Showtime at the Apollo*, young Black comics didn't have a national outlet. Martin won the first round and lost in the next round. But some producer saw him and put him on the TV show *What's Happening Now*. It was going to air at 6 a.m. and Martin would be on it. As you'll hear me say, I was always proud of D.C. comics and supported them. So at 6 a.m. there I was, in front of the TV watching Martin on *What's Happening Now*. I couldn't believe someone I knew was on national TV.

In June 1989, I had an opportunity to go to L.A. to see Tommy Davidson shooting the first episode of *In Living Color*, and I jumped on it. As I was chilling in Tommy's dressing room, Martin came in. I was happy to see him. He said he was working on a movie called *House Party*. He told me to leave DC behind and come to Hollywood and make it happen. I told him I would within one year, which I did. The next time I saw Martin was at the Comedy Act Theatre in 1990, where he was showcasing for someone. I had just moved to L.A. and was making my rounds to all of the comedy clubs. I was actually doing well. After the showcase, Martin came up to me and told me there was a part in *House Party 2* that I should go out for. But in the same breath he said, "I shouldn't be giving you any info 'cause I heard you been talking shit about me" and walked off. I stood there dumbfounded. I truly didn't understand. I thought, *"Motherfucker, I got nothing but love for you. I woke up at 6 a.m. to watch yo monkey-ass, I went to see yo pre-screening HBO special, I let everyone know you from DC and you say this bullshit?"* I tried to think of what I could have said. Then I thought about a moment when I was performing at that club weeks earlier and Joe Torry (who was a close friend of Martin's) was hosting. I had rocked the house and Joe went up onstage and said, "Give it up for Pierre! I'll give him an 'A' for being Funny and a 'D' for Originality." I was thinking, *"What the fuck is he talking about?"* So when he got off stage I approached him to see what was up. He said I did a joke Martin had been doing, so I must have stolen it from him. I said, "How do you know Martin didn't steal it from me?" The joke wasn't the exactly the same. I told Joe if Martin had a problem with that then HE should come say something. Meaning *"I don't need to hear shit from yo ass."* I guessed that's what Martin was referring to, because I couldn't think of anything else. Martin and I haven't been cool ever since.

When I did *Def Comedy Jam Season 1*, Martin was the host. Comics going on the show would have to tell Martin their intro and he would say it onstage. At the time I was twenty-three and the youngest headlining comic in the country. I think Martin was only a year older and was doing much better than me, BUT I was the youngest headlining comic, so I asked him to say that in my intro. He flatly said no. I thought that was fucked up. It hurt only because I looked up to this brother. That was the last time I would look up to him. He changed me. Knowing him personally and seeing his success made me feel like you can't help your competition. And I would try many times to be like that, but I just wasn't raised that way. I am and have always been into helping others. So watch the first time I was on *Def Comedy Jam*. That intro was what HE wanted to say.

I would go on to see him hit levels of success in entertainment very few would ever reach. With him being from D.C., I will always have love for him. We may not connect on a friendship level, but that doesn't mean I can't be a fan of his work.

Martin Lawrence and my manager Ron -In Tommy Davidson's dressing room on the set of *In Living Color*

Master P *(Rapper, Mogul)*

It was late 1998. I heard that P was filming around my neighborhood in LA at a club called the Congo Lounge, which was owned by Jennifer Lopez. He was filming the movie *Foolish* with Eddie Griffin, whose career was really hot at the time. The director, Dave Meyers, was a fan of mine so I figured I would pop my head in on the set and say "what's up." When I got on the set it was nighttime, and I noticed they had more security than the President. I mean everywhere you looked, someone had a gun. I was mad that I didn't bring my shyt (just joking). I think since Master P was so hot then and they were filming in L.A., they felt they didn't want any gang problems.

When I arrived on the set, someone (I forgot who) wanted to introduce me to P. They brought me around to the back of the club where the trailers were. We started to chop it up, and P said he wanted to work with me on a few movies. Just then, a commotion broke out because one of the extra actors had a gun on him. My meeting with P was brief.

I ran into him again in the summer of 1999 at the Universal Amphitheatre in LA. He had a comedy show called *Master P's Comedy All Stars*, which he ended up making a DVD out of. I was backstage and I saw him surrounded by a ton of people (remember he was hot then). When I got to him we spoke, and he told he wanted to work with me someday.

The next time I saw him was at the Acapulco Black Film Festival in Mexico, where my own movie *For Da Love of Money* was being screened. He was receiving an award for something (making bad movies possibly?) I can't be mad at him because they gave him a gold Rolex. I saw him at the pool with his entourage one morning and again he said he wanted to work with me, so I told him to get at me when he was ready to write the check.

Another time I ran into P was when a casting director friend of mine, Phaedra Harris, called me and said she was on set with Master P and he wanted me to come down and be in the movie. I wasn't doing anything that day so why not see what this was about? I drove to the Valley in L.A. and came upon the set and the crew. They were headquartered at an old mall. It was a Sunday so it was very slow. Phaedra and I had lunch on the set and she took me over to the filming area where P was working in this little house. There was this guy filming all the behind-the-scenes footage and P asked if I would do a little shout out about the set. I saw no harm in that, so I went off the set, signed a release form and the camera man had me sit in a car and do my piece. It was quick and easy.

I watched a little more of the filming and saw how low-budget everything was. I decided not to wait around in case they were trying to give me a part in this movie. Now don't get me wrong, I'm down with a film no matter what the budget is; but the lower the budget, the better the movie needs to be.

A few years later I was at some club and this young cat approached me and said he was a fan. He told me he had just seen me in a Master P movie. I told him he was mistaken. I know a lot of the urban movies seem similar, but I never was in a Master P movie. It turned out that I was in one. Remember the little bullshyt I did in the car? This nicca put that in the film, somewhere in the intro. I can't even be mad at P for that move, he caught me slipping.

Master P is a true hustler and you gotta respect that. Now if he can just hustle his way into some acting classes, we all will be straight...(laugh). *(See photo)*

Max Julien *(Actor)*

It was August 1996, and the third week of filming *How to Be A Player*. There was an air of excitement on the set because Max Julien (from *The Mack*) was filming that day. Now I had heard of him, but believe it or not I hadn't seen *The Mack* (a Cardinal sin in the hood). When it came time to shoot my scene with him, I remember coming from my trailer and walking up to the table and Max was holding court with like six cast and crew members. He was kicking knowledge like he WAS *The Mack*, so I pulled up a chair. This man is smooth; he should have been a real pimp. I remember thinking how good looking this man was for his age (no homo). He had a full head of hair, smooth skin, all of his teeth and he was pushing fifty-three years old. I can see why all the ladies dug him in the 70's. Hell, there are some who still dig him today. All I know is I wouldn't mind looking like that at that age. Making movies can be chaotic; people yelling, running around, a lot of tension. But not for Max. Through all the chaos, while people were running around trying to get the shot ready, he kept his composure as if filmmaking was minor. I really admired that about him. I've seen even established actors get nervous right before the director yells action. From that day on, I took a page from his book and I don't let anything about filmmaking bother me. Like I said, I had heard about him but I hadn't done any research on him. So all I could do was listen. Well I got his phone number, went home and did my homework on him and was blown away. This man is a pioneer in Black cinema. He has starred in some classic Black films, as well as wrote, directed and produced many films. He's even been involved in filmmaking overseas. This man is truly a Black national treasure. I stayed in touch with him for the next few years. I even called him for advice when I was about to film *For Da Love of Money* and he graciously gave me advice. Max is the man, always ready to help a young artist. Any young artist or filmmaker should do their homework on this brother. Big Ups to Max.

Mekhi Phifer *(Actor)*

I first met Mekhi at the Melrose Improv Comedy Club on Mo' Betta Monday a.k.a "Black" night. We were in the lobby and he was about to snatch some dude up, for what I believe was something to do with his lady. All I know is he was in this dude's face and snatched this dude by the collar and was about to unleash a can of whoop ass, when one of his boys grabbed him and ushered him away. I was like, that's my type of dude! Show them that acting is just your job. We chopped it up a little outside the club and parted ways. Years later I ran into him in Arizona at a celebrity giveaway party during Superbowl weekend. We were chilling with a good friend of mine named Ronnie Warner, who he did the movie *Puff Puff Pass* with. We laughed about how we were getting all this free shit and we weren't anything but dudes from the city. Mekhi is a real dude. He seemed like the kind of guy you wouldn't mind hanging out with.

Mike Epps *(Comic, Actor)*

I met Mike around the comedy circuit. I always thought he was funny on a street level. He was that dude on the corner that would do whatever, be down for whatever and always have everyone tripping. The thing that I liked about Mike was that when he was on, he'd be on (funny as hell), but when he wasn't, he wasn't. He went on stage with the truest of emotions, never faking. If he felt good that night, then that night you got a great show. If he was mad about something that night. Well, that's what you got.

In 1994 I had saved up a little bit of money and wanted to shoot a movie of my own, *The Company You Keep*. It was about four friends who go out one night and stumble up on a dead body. With them being around the scene of the crime, they were fingered for the murder. But before the cops came, they escaped back to their neighborhood and their friendships fell apart throughout the ongoing investigation. Well I wanted Mike to play the part of the wild one of the four friends. I asked Mike if he was interested and he was. He was excited, and so was I because I could tell Mike was going to be a star one day. And I'd be giving him his first movie role.

As I was getting things prepared for the film (castings, locations, etc.), a very close comedian friend of mine who I had shared the news with informed me that while he was on tour with Mike, he had gotten really high a few times and sometimes wasn't up to par when it came to performing. The next time I saw Mike out at a club I approached him, pulled him to the side and explained to him, "I still want you in my movie, but I heard you do certain things. I'm spending all the money I have to do this movie and I can't afford you not to be on top of your game." Mike proceeded to get loud, telling me to "get the fuck outta my face with that bullshit," "who the fuck said that," "you better not come to me with no bullshit." Now I tried to calm him down but he was getting louder and a few people started to notice. So I asked him to come around the corner with me, because I was about to find out how well he could box. I wanted him to see that I had a little talent too. It never came to that. For the next couple of months we would see each other and not speak. One night at a comedy club, he approached me and said he had no hard feelings and we squashed it. I never made that movie, but I know he would have been great in it. He went on to movie stardom.

Over the years we've shared the stage many times. We're cool now. He has gone on to see success, which I'm happy for. Can't nobody tell me I don't have an eye for raw talent.

Mike Epps- After our concert in Miami

Mike Tyson *(Boxer)*

I was living in Arizona and there was a live fight night at the Celebrity Theatre. You know how much I like boxing, so you know I was there. Before the fights started, I noticed a crowd gathering on the other side of the theatre. A friend of mine, who ran the gym I worked out in, told me that it was Mike Tyson and that we should go say hi. So I grabbed my ears (just joking). We went over there and I introduced myself. I was pleasantly surprised by how engaging and cool he was. Hey, I'm just like everyone else. All I had seen or heard was what was in the media. We sat next to him and his trainer and watched the fights. He signed quite a few autographs, more than he should have because it caused him to be interrupted during the fights. I feel a certain way about autographs. I really don't mind signing them, in fact I love signing them, but not in the middle of me doing something. Catch me leaving a spot or while I'm chilling, and I got you.

After the fight we all decided to go to a club. Mike and his friend drove ahead while we followed behind them. At one point we stopped at a convenience store; Mike and his friend went in and I followed. He seemed to be a little high, but then again I had never met the dude so that just might have been how he was. But I was struck by his size. He wasn't that big, and me being a weekend boxer and all, I thought for a moment I wouldn't mind getting in the ring with him. Then I snapped to my senses and paid for my juice. Hey, this was 2005 Tyson who hadn't fought in a long time and he had lost the last couple fights. But I was also 2005 comedian Pierre, and he would have killed me.

We got to the club and sat in VIP. He was telling us how women don't talk to him anymore, how they all thought he was crazy and seemed to be afraid of him. But it was funny the way he was telling us about it. All I could think about was how far from grace he had fallen; this man used to be the king of the world and now he was telling us how things had turned out. But he truly seemed to have come to grips with where he was in life. Sometimes things seem better when you're rich and powerful. But when it's over, you're so relieved that the pressure is gone. After an hour or so, my friend and I said our goodbyes and went home.

Mike would go on to have resurgence in his life with his cameo in the movie *The Hangover*, and the documentary, *Tyson.* As far as I'm concerned, Mike is alright with me.

Monique *(Comic, Actress)*

I had been hearing about Monique for years in Maryland. She's from Baltimore, which is about thirty minutes north of where I grew up. When I left for Hollywood in the early 90's, she and her brother ran a comedy club, which back then was a rarity. No comics ran a comedy club, except for Steve Harvey. The only bad thing about her club was that she and her brother never hired me. I felt slighted. I mean, they hired damn near every other comic in the area. So I never had any desire to meet her. Until one night in the early 90's, she was outside the Comedy Store with her brother/manager. She was in Hollywood because some network was trying to give her a talk show of her own. She was so warm and friendly, that I knew me not working with her wasn't personal, but just a case of 'out of sight, out of mind' since I had moved to L.A. I was so happy that she might be getting a show. As I always say, I'm so proud when an artist from the Washington, D.C., area makes it.

I saw her again around 1998 when we both were guests on a late night show on BET hosted by John Salley. She was a star on *The Parkers* at that time. I wouldn't run into her again until years later at a party. She invited me to her house in the Valley for a small get together. When I got to her house (which was surprisingly only eight houses down from my manager's), I was taken aback by how small it was. The front of the house wasn't kept up. I mean, she had been on TV for years and touring. I thought maybe she and her husband might be saving up for another place. Her house seemed very normal, nothing really expensive inside from what I could see. Now what she did have was a lot of kids running around, doing hair, watching TV and playing cards on the back porch. The atmosphere was that of someone with a nine-to-five job, not a Hollywood star. Monique greeted me like I was someone she knew all her life. She told me to just come in and fit in where I fit in, that I was on my own. Which was cool but a little strange. I joined it like I was at home, but after a few hours I had to make another run. Monique is the same in front of the camera as she is behind it. You have to give credit where credit is due. She has what it takes to be a STAR. What impresses me even more is that she doesn't look like a typical star that Hollywood cranks out, but she still became one.

The next time I ran into her was in November 2009 when she was all the rage in Hollywood. She had the Oscar buzz (which she would eventually win) and she had the hottest show on BET. She had me as a guest on her late night show. I felt really relaxed on her show, which made many people think I did a great job that night. But I give all the credit to her. When she and I get in a room together, it's like kicking with one of my D.C. homies. It was good to see her after all these years. As soon as I could, I checked her out in Precious and she did her thing. Who says talent doesn't come out of the D.C. area?

What I respect about Monique so much is that she has done it her way, and when I say her way, I mean *her way*. She is everything you see: loveable, loud, sassy, real, edgy, and sweet.

(See photo)

Muhammad Ali *(Boxer)*

My best friend Joe P. and I were driving in LA in the summer of 2000, when we came to a stop sign and I noticed May-May Ali (Muhammad Ali's daughter, *not* the boxer) walking down the sidewalk. I had first met her at the *Comedy Store* where she was doing stand up comedy. She asked if I would like to meet her father. Now y'all know I'm a huge boxing fan. That was like asking RuPaul if he likes eye shadow! Muhammad was in a building nearby signing posters. I told her to give me a minute and I would be right back. I ran to a drugstore and got a disposable camera. I went to the building and entered an office that had a lot of sports memorabilia in it. And there was Muhammad Ali sitting at a desk, signing posters. He was being assisted by who I believe was another daughter (again, not the boxer). I thought he only had two daughters. But then again, I don't know his personal history just his professional history. He was frail, not the Ali I remember from his fighting days. But still there was the Champ. May-May told me to stand next to him and take a photo. I had Joe take it. I can't lie, I was excited. This was Muhammad Ali. Forget if he wasn't in top form. This man is history. I stayed a few more minutes and thanked May-May and left. Do you know I never got that picture developed? I didn't want to develop just one picture in a new camera (me being cheap) and years later when I found the camera, it had expired. I didn't know film expired. Damn. But I know I met the champ and that's all that matters.

Musiq Soulchild *(Singer)*

I first met Musiq in 2002 at the Arena Theatre in Houston. I was his opening act. I remember hating doing the show because I had to perform on a stage that was in a circle and moved during the performance. The stage was full of equipment and he wanted it to look romantic; so he had a couch, lamp and table on stage too. There was way too much stuff on stage to make me feel comfortable. I had to step around all that shit to do my act. But hey the show wasn't about me. I shouldn't be complaining; I was getting $5,000 for fifteen minutes so fuck it, make that money.

I was in my dressing room which was next to his and connected with an adjoining door. I opened my door and he was sitting there with a few folks, without his glasses on. I didn't know he was damn near cross-eyed! I introduced myself to him and he was very cordial. A very humble brother. It was time for him to perform, so I decided to catch his act. A funny thing happened during his performance that night. He was doing his thing and was getting the ladies all riled up, when he decided he'd jump on top of the table and sing. Well that table wasn't meant for him to stand on and it broke in two and he came crashing down! But dude popped back up, never missing a beat, and kept singing like nothing happened. People's mouths were wide open thinking he had to have had broken something. Musiq is a true pro. He put on a great show that night. I didn't realize how many great songs he has.

I ran into him again backstage when I working at *The Essence* festival in Houston in 2006. I was sitting in the VIP section and it was really dark. Someone said hi to me and I gave them a hi back, not really paying attention who it was because I had to get ready to work. I didn't want to come off like I was brushing this person off so I looked back, and I noticed it was Musiq. I stopped and told him what a fan I was of him, and how much I would love working with him again. I told him that was a great idea, and to make it happen.

The next time I saw him, I was in Atlanta rehearsing for a play called *Loving Him is Killing Me* in April 2010. It was while I was finishing up this book. This time I got a few minutes to chop it up with him. We laughed about the show we did together in 2002. He was on his way to South Africa for a tour and I told him I had toured there myself a few times. I had gone to a city in South Africa that he wanted to go to but wasn't because of a shady promoter. I thought, *"Wow, even on his level he has to deal with shady promoters."* This business is crazy. I have become a big fan of his, not just as a performer but as a person. To me, he's very underrated. I know the feeling.

Mystikal *(Rapper)*

I was living in Dallas in October 2001 when a club owner invited me to Club Prime to check out Mystikal. I had heard his music before and read a few articles on him in hip-hop magazines. I felt like from what I read that he was a cool person, and I liked the fact he had been in the military. When someone has done something different as an adult before they became successful in the entertainment business, it is always interesting to me. It makes me feel like maybe they had second thoughts. I have known what I wanted to do since I was sixteen years old; I had minor jobs in my lifetime, but nothing that lasted more than a year, and nothing I wasn't ready to walk away from at a moment's notice. Because I had my mind focused on becoming a star.

I arrived at the club and it was packed beyond capacity. The stage was so packed, Mystikal didn't even have space to perform (most club promoters don't give a damn about safety; they want that money!). I was looking forward to seeing him perform because, like many, I had become a fan of his music. He came out and the crowd went NUTS. I forget what song he came out to, but all of his music is hype. He did a few songs and before he could complete his set, the fire marshal shut the place down and many ran out and left. I ended up out in the parking lot looking for my car. I found my car and as I was leaving, I passed a limo and saw that someone had their head out, yelling at ladies walking by. Then out of the limo I heard someone say towards me, "Oh shit, that's my man." I stopped and Mystikal stuck his head out and told me he was a fan. I told him the same. We exchanged phone numbers and I met a few of the local rappers who I would befriend. We went our separate ways. I don't hang out after a club closes down. That's when fools start acting a fool.

A few months later I was in Memphis hanging out when I heard Mystikal was performing at Isaac Hayes' club. I went to catch his show and say to say hi. The club was packed (you've got to remember, he was HOT at this time). I tried to get backstage but security was trippin'. Why do some of these folks try to overdo their jobs? Look, without these stars, you'd be back at the gym trying to sign up new members. Someone who worked directly with Mystikal saw me, and told me to give him one minute. A few seconds later I walked past security smiling. Mystikal embraced me when I got back there and we exchanged numbers once more because I had lost his. His show was hype as usual. We talked about hooking up with a few honeys after the show, but I had someone with me. So I knew that wasn't going down.

A few years later I was in a play, *Something She Can Feel,* and there was a part where we needed a musical performer. We originally had Charlie Wilson (from the Gap Band), but he was working on his album and wouldn't be available for some of the dates. So I suggested Mystikal as a replacement to the producers and they liked the idea. I called him and he came through. Our first show date together was in Knoxville, Tennessee. I met him in the hotel (I had already been there for a few days). He was eager to do a little acting, and he was real cool to work with.

His part in the play was as the entertainment that a rich family had hired for a party they were having at their house. When Mystikal was announced and he broke into his raps, you should have seen the looks of some of the audience members' faces (*remember, these plays get more of the gospel crowd*). Some were in shock and some stood up and got their groove on. Others had that look of "*I would never!*" I was onstage dancing and laughing my ass off. Mystikal was a straight pro. He performed like everyone was into him. He even threw money out into the audience during his performances. You should see how those "church" folk acted when money was thrown. No different than "heathens,"

One night after a show, my best friend Joe P, Big Reg, Mystikal and I were called to a cast member's room, and he had a fine ass, thick, big booty having young lady in his room who was willing to do...let's say, whatever Mystikal and I wanted. I ain't gonna lie, I thought about it; but we were going to a club and were running late, plus I was rolling too deep and all those fools would have wanted to partake in the activities. And I didn't know Mystikal like that. We left Mystikal and the cast mate (I won't mention his name because he was married) in the room. I never found out what happened when I left, but I know what would have happened if I had stayed. But hey, that's me. Charlie Wilson ended up coming back to the play the next day. Mystikal did a few more shows during the tour and he was always cool and very generous with his money. If we went out, Mystikal would pay for everyone.

When I heard the news of Mystikal's arrest for rape, I was hurt, not because I thought he did it, but just the opposite. I truly don't believe he did it (true, I wasn't there) but the man I was around, that wasn't even in his character. If I would have felt even a slight feeling of this dude being grimy, I would have stepped when I first met him. I believe he could have been set up or he put himself in a situation he shouldn't have been around, and with people who didn't have his best interests at heart. If I had been there, that would have never had gone down. No sex is worth losing everything you have worked so hard for.

I wrote him a few times while he was in jail but never got a response. But my boy Big Reg stayed in contact with him and would always give me a report on how he was doing. He's out of jail now and he's someone I'm pulling for, because he's a good dude. I was in Memphis in late May 2010, and my phone rang. It was Mystikal. He said he received my letter and apologized for not returning it. I told him to stay out of trouble, and I'd catch him somewhere around the country.

New Edition *(Singing Group)*

It was June 1998 and promoter, Al Haymon, would send me out on tour with different musical acts. He asked if I would like to open up for NE on their *"Home Again"* tour. They had to end a tour they were on a year earlier because of Bobby Brown. Word had it that Bobby would bring Whitney Houston and their baby onstage and sometimes during the group's performance. Bobby would sing damn near all of all his own songs, even though each group member was only supposed to sing a fraction of each of their own songs. So they gave Bobby the boot, recorded a new album and went on tour without him.

My first show with them was in Oakland at a theatre. I flew myself up there from L.A., got myself a hotel room and went straight to the theatre. I ran into Ricky Bell first in the hallway and clicked with him really quickly. I told him that I was a big fan of him and his group and he told me he was a fan of mine (as usual, I was surprised that he even knew me). I found him to be really humble and down to earth. Ronnie, Mike and Ralph were also cool. Johnny was cool, but you could tell he had a little "star" thing going about himself.

I went to the dressing rooms, where Ralph was calling out to some young girls. I reminded him of a time when I saw him in South Carolina at a hole-in-the-wall club while he was promoting that *"Sensitivity"* song. We both laughed at some of the places we have had to perform in.

I went onstage and had a good show. There were so many fine young ladies there. Even though they hadn't had a new hit in many years, it was good to see their fans still come out to support. After I got finished I walked out into the lobby while they performed and some people were complaining to me that Bobby wasn't on the show. Some even said they wanted their money back. I thought, *"Why are you telling me this? I can't do nothing fo ya"*... It's a shame that people complained because they put on such a great show.

It's cool when you befriend celebrities you grew up on. I can still remember the first time I heard *"Candy Girl."* It seems like it was just twenty-eight years ago. I ran into Ricky a few times after that at parties in L.A. We always have a good laugh about those days.

Nick Cannon *(Actor)*

I would see Nick around the Melrose Improv Comedy Club on Mo' Betta Mondays in the mid 90's. He had a manager I knew, who was a cool dude. Nick was always trying to get onstage, but he was only about fifteen years old; and when he did get onstage, he was sillier than he was funny. But I had to give him props for even getting up there. I think I was drawn to him because he reminded me of myself. I was seventeen years old when I started. He was also part of a rap duo from San Diego around this time.

Nick once opened up for me in Alaska (he was on *Nickelodeon* at the time) this was his first time traveling doing comedy and he was really excited. The first night we arrived we took him to his first strip club, he looked like a kid in the candy store. (lol) The next night at the show he opened the show. He was much funnier then he had been since I last saw him at the clubs, and he did really well in front of a mature crowd. I remember watching from offstage thinking, this boy has something. His timing was very good and he seemed very comfortable on stage. He was a natural and the crowd loved him, especially the young ladies. Later that that evening I was chilling back in my hotel room when I got a knock at the door. I looked through the peephole and saw two females. I thought, *"Damn, it's like that in Alaska?"* I opened the door and they asked me where Nick was. I told them he was next door as I shut the door. I knew then Nick was going to be a star.

A few years later I had a meeting with some agents, and all they could talk about was Nick Cannon: how he had just done this movie *Drumline* and how he was going to be a star. I thought, *"That's all good but this meeting is supposed to be about ME."*

While I was doing a play in Chicago, *Something She Can Feel*. I ran into him at a restaurant. He came over and we sat and ate together. He told me he was there working with R. Kelly on a record. We parted ways as he got into his waiting limo and I walked back to my hotel.

I got a call from his assistant once when I was returning into town from a long flight, saying that Nick personally wanted me to watch him tape his new show. I was too tired and passed on the invitation. The show was *Wildin' Out*. I've seen him many times since then and we've always had good words. I know people think he's corny and soft, but he's one of the coolest young actors in the business. Don't sleep on him-he hasn't had all his success because he's *not* a smart businessman. I wish him all the success. Now how he got Mariah? Well, that boggles my mind too. But then again, Bobby got Whitney…

Omarion *(Singer)*

In the mid 90's, I used to get my hair cut at this barbershop in Hollywood where Omarion's mother braided hair. I would always see him there sweeping up the hair on the floor. He was around thirteen years old, and I remember he had a lot of energy.

One day I took him to the Popeye's Chicken next door to the shop, and talked to him about his dream of being an actor, girls, etc. When I got him away from his mother, I got to see another side of him. He was a bit cocky, which I liked. I knew he would need that to make it in the business. He was a nice looking little dude with a lot of personality, and his hair was always nicely braided, thanks to his mother. You don't usually see little thirteen year old boys with their hair neatly braided every single day! So I knew he might start getting in trouble with girls. He kind of reminded me of myself at that age. So I knew what he might be in for! After eating we went back to the shop. I would see him periodically in the shop after that. One day I was watching TV and a cereal commercial came on. I was like, "that's the little dude from the shop! He's on his way!" Soon after that, B2K was formed and well, the rest is history.

I took my daughter to see B2K in concert one night, and my hearing has never been the same since. That night I could tell that Omarion had too much personality and charisma to stay in a group. We went backstage after the show to meet the group. As soon as Omarion saw me, he gave me a big hug and we talked and laughed about the days when he used to sweep up hair in the barbershop.

So, my assessment of him was right. As I watch his career flourish now, I am proud of him. He ain't the little boy in the barbershop anymore.

P. Diddy *(Rapper, Mogul)*

I was backstage the *Budweiser Super Fest Tour*, walking through the hallways during the show. Out of nowhere, a crew of like ten dudes came walking through. I thought, *"Who the hell is this? I know all the stars on this show and none of them are rolling like that.*" Right in the middle of them all was Diddy. He recognized me and said, *"that's a funny guy right there."* I'm always known as *"that funny dude,"* never Pierre. Hey, it's cool; at least they recognize my skills.

The next time I seen him was in our management office in LA he was coming through to speak to Benny Medina and we said a few words.

What I like about Diddy is that he knows how to make an entrance. In Hollywood, you have to set yourself apart and he's mastered how to do that. You gotta give him props for that. What I admire about him so much is that this dude ain't great at shyt: rapping, producing, acting, you name it, but he's great at making us believe he is. Many people don't have that quality. He has mastered the art of showmanship. I'd have Diddy on my team any day.

I've recently saw him in the movie *Get Him to the Greek* and he did a really good job. They say he was playing himself. (lol)

Go 'head Diddy, I can respect your hustle. If they're buying, sell it.

Patti Labelle *(Singer)*

After I toured with the *Budweiser Super Fest Tour* in early 1998, promoter Al Haymon gave me a few dates to open up for some of the artists whose tours he was promoting. One of them happened to be Patti LaBelle. I was backstage in my dressing room at the Universal Amphitheatre in L.A., when I heard this voice coming from outside my room. It was one of those voices, full of energy. I opened the door to find Patti directing a few guys where to put some trays of food. Tours usually have some pretty good food catered in, but nothing like when Patti's got time to make some food.

I walked out and said hi. The tour manager told her that I was her opening act. She gave me a big hug and said, *"Baby, you go get some of Momma's (her) homemade food."* I was shocked that she treated me like I was real family. I didn't even trip that this was Patti LaBelle, one of the GREATEST female singers of all time! I went into the room where the food was. There was so much food and it looked so good, a nicca thought it was Thanksgiving! After I ate I wanted to have a great show, not only for me, but also for her. I was no longer just an individual on the show. I felt like family.

I went out and had a good show, but not great. For some reason some of my jokes didn't hit the way they usually hit. I'm used to people rolling in the aisles laughing! I was confused; I mean, I put my best material out there! Now by no means did I stink that night. I was just used to killing, having people doubling over, sides hurting, and tears rolling, especially when I was the only comic. I later found out later that Patti has a lot of gay fans, so my relationship jokes about dating women and want women do, weren't flying that night. "Excuuuse me! No he didn't!" So the next time I worked with her, I changed my material up and little bit and killed.

I would go out into the audience sometimes and watch Patti perform. You're talking about a pro! From the moment she stepped on that stage, she looked like a star. She wore a form fitting dress that highlighted her shape. She would give some of these young girls a run for their money! The diamonds she had on would have *re*-blinded Stevie Wonder. I couldn't help but look at those damn diamonds, around her neck, wrist and fingers. She was killing it. She looked like Gucci Mane and Plies' mama! (But classy). She called a young man on stage and sang to him on a little couch. She danced, flirted with the audience, and sang until she damn near passed out. All I can say is, Patti puts on a show. Every time I worked with her she brought her "A" game. If you are a young singer, you need to catch her live. Patti is damn near seventy years old and still would put a hurtin' on some of these young divas, who just walk back and forth across the stage and call that putting on a show. Patti is the true essence of an R&B legend.

Paul Mooney *(Comic, Writer)*

I first saw Paul back on Oct 20, 1987, as the opening act for Eddie Murphy's *Lord Have Murphy* tour at the Capitol Center in Maryland. I had just been shot a few days earlier and still had a cast on my arm. But I was still excited to see Eddie. I was going to see him by any means necessary. I was still young in comedy at the time, so to me, Eddie was a comedy god. The first guy to hit the stage was some comic who had a long pole across his shoulder with six life-sized puppets on it, and they did a dance routine. I thought, *"OK, bring on Eddie."* After Puppet man got done, another comic walked on and I thought, *"oh great, ANOTHER act before Eddie."* This was when I first saw Paul Mooney. The moment he opened his mouth, I knew he was different from any comic I'd ever seen. His cockiness, arrogance, and confidence had me hooked. I sat up in my seat. All I could think was *"who is this guy talking all this shit on stage, and having people laughing at shit they surely shouldn't be??"* He was talking about racism, White people, and the government. I couldn't believe it! In a regular conversation, that shyt would get someone an ass whooping! At that moment I told myself that I should say whatever I want on stage. But it's not what you say, it's how you say it. Let me tell you something though, saying what you want is a heavy burden to carry and many times I've tossed and turned about what I was doing on stage. Everyone can't say what they're *really* thinking. It may look easy but trust me, it ain't.

I first met Paul in person at the Comedy Store around 1994, where we would work together nightly. I would watch his humor run all the White people out of the club. Because of this, they would put him on last. After the shows, I would stand in the corner in the hallway and watch him interact with fans and how at times, he would brush people off. I would stand back and take it all in. Sometimes when I was performing, he'd come watch me from the doorway. I once told him he was like *"the masturbation of comedy."* He asked what that meant and I said "everyone enjoys it but nobody wants to admit to doing it." He laughed hard and said, *"Oh, oh you're too funny! Oh homey, you're so right. That's a good one. Say it again!"* Then he said to himself, *"the masturbation of comedy, everyone enjoys it but no one wants to admit to it. I like that homey, that's gooood."*

I saw how Paul would interact with White people opposed to Black people. He would give White people a little more time and I called him on it. I said *"Mooney, you ain't all that pro-Black. I'ma start calling you Paul Cooney!"* and he just laughed and laughed. He said, *"Oh that's funny! Oh, you see me working over here. You got your eye on me, huh homey?"* I said all this with the upmost respect for Mr. Mooney. Every night he performed, I would wait to watch him, even if it meant waiting two or three hours. For some, watching Mooney was therapeutic, and at times I needed my therapy. Let's be real, this is a screwed up world we live in. And he reports it all.

Years later I was trying to get booked at Caroline's on Broadway in New York City and was having a hard time. One weekend I was there in New York to see some friends, and I saw that Mooney would be at Caroline's. So I decided to stop by. While I was there, Mooney told the owner about me and the next thing I knew, I was working at that club and would for years. A lot of people don't know that Mooney has a caring side that he keeps hidden.

One time I happened to be back home in D.C. and Mooney was performing at the Improv downtown. So I decided to stop through to watch Mooney. We linked up after the show and he told me that he was going to New York the next day to handle some business. I told him I was heading there myself the next day to start my week performing at Caroline's. We agreed to meet at the train station and ride up to New York together. The next day I got to the train station and didn't see Mooney, but I knew he was coming so I decided to get my ticket. I bought one in first class, because I wanted to sit with Mr. Mooney. As I boarded the train and walked back to first class, the bartender stopped me and said, "I see all the comics are on here." I asked where Mooney was and he pointed to the coach section. You mean I bought a first class seat and this nicca is riding COACH? All I could do was laugh.

I saw him just sitting there by himself. He saw me and gave me that *"I'm surprised you made it nigga"* look and I sat next to him. We made some small talk and I started to dig into Mooney's brain. He is a fiercely private person to those he doesn't know. Dude has some trust issues. I can't blame him; Hollywood can do that to you. But Paul likes me, so he started to open up about his experiences in Hollywood and some of the stories were crazy! He would go on years later to write a book, which I read. He left out many of those stories.

After the three-hour train trip, we exited Penn Station in New York City and as quickly as we said hello, we said goodbye. He went his way and I went mine. That's classic Mooney: *"enjoy me while I'm here because when I'm gone, I'm gone and don't ask me to return."*

I would see him from time to time, even share the same stage with him. As I was writing this book, I thought of one person and one person only to write the foreword: Paul Mooney. If you don't know Mooney, he can come off as an asshole or stuck up. Which he is, but once you understand him or he let's you peek into his world you'll see that Mooney is one of a kind and you can deal with him or not.

(See photo)

Queen Latifah *(Rapper, Actress)*

In 1999, I hosted Russell Simmons' TV show, *"One World Music Beat."* I would read entertainment news and do funny commentary with it. Queen Latifah was starring in a movie, *Bones,* at the time with Denzel Washington. I made a sexual orientation joke about her not liking a "bone." Hey, I'm a comic! But I later realized if you ain't sure about something that sensitive, it's best not to say anything. I went on rumors and not first hand experience.

I saw her in 2000 in Nashville, Tennessee, at the Grand Ole Opry house for a music convention. I was there to look for musical artists for the soundtrack for my movie *For Da Love of Money.* As I was wading through the thick crowd of musical artists, wannabe's, and groupies (both men and women), I saw Latifah walk past me so I stopped her and said hey. She looked at me and said, "I heard what you said about me." At that moment I felt so small. But then she said "it's cool" and I quickly apologized and she walked off.

There's a lesson here, which I took as 'be careful what you say, even in jest, about someone's personal life. You never know who'll hear about it or how they may take it. Fortunately, she was cool enough to let it roll off her back. That's why she's the Queen.

Quentin Tarantino *(Director)*

In the fall of 1996, I was called by casting director Jaki Brown-Karman to audition for a new Quentin Tarantino movie called *Jackie Brown*, starring Samuel L. Jackson, Robert DeNiro, and Pam Grier. My name was hot and being circulated throughout the business, so I started auditioning for bigger movies. I read the script and knew I had this; I could feel it. I was to play this little dope fiend named Beaumont Livingston that Samuel Jackson would kill. I thought, *"I'm moving up to the big time now. I'm getting killed by a well-respected actor. I guess a gay role is coming next."* (No pun intended.)

I came to the audition focused. I was dressed for the part, and even had a fake joint. Jaki called me into the room with Quentin and his producer, Lawrence Bender. Now Jaki was a big fan of mine, she was the casting director on *How to Be a Player*. I entered the room confidently (when I'm prepared, not many can compete with me) and did the usual greetings. Quentin said he'd act the opposite role with me while I auditioned. Now I'm a huge Quentin Tarantino fan, but at that moment all the adoration was gone. He was just a dude I was reading with. I was too focused. I remember him asking me if I was ready, and in two seconds I went from being dressed like a normal guy to taking a few things off and standing there with a wife beater, doo rag, sagging pants, two beepers and a joint in my mouth. Looking like a dope fiend. He was taken aback by the effort I had put in.

We started reading the scene and I was killing it. He even asked to hit my fake joint, and he added the word *"nigga"* in places that wasn't in the script. I guess at that moment, I was Dat Nicca. I even ad-libbed for like two minutes after the end of the scene. When we were done, I knew I had this part. I was *Dat Nicca*. As I left the audition, everyone was congratulating me. Jaki smiled at me as she walked me out, and I left that audition on a high. The next day, my manager called Jaki and she said they loved me, and that I was the favorite for the part. They would make their decision in a week, but she felt like I had it. I was on cloud nine. For the next week all I could do was think about being in that movie.

I had to perform stand-up out of town the next weekend, and on my red-eye flight back home, I ran into Gabriel Cassius (*Fallen, Buffalo Soldiers*) and I told him about the movie. He said he heard about that movie, with Samuel L. Jackson, Robert DeNiro and Chris Tucker. Hold up. Chris Tucker? I thought about the script and thought, there was no part in that movie that Chris could play, except for the one I went out for. I got quiet. The plane couldn't fly fast enough. As soon as I landed I called my manager and he broke the news. He said he didn't want to tell me and ruin my show out of town. I thought, *"Why would Chris want that small part? I mean he had his own starring role in Money Talks!"* I would later find out that he just wanted to be in a movie with that caliber of stars. I can't be mad at him. "Big bank takes little bank."

So, I never got a chance to work with one of my favorite directors. But I can say that in the fall of 1996, I got a chance to impress him.

R. Kelly *(Singer)*

I believe the year was 1992. A management company ran by Barry Hankerson (Aaliyah's uncle) was looking at me for possible work. I was performing at the comedy club, All Jokes Aside, in Chicago. They came out to see me and brought R. Kelly with them. I had a great show and we went out to celebrate. I ended up riding solo with R. Kelly in his Jeep Cherokee for the evening.

Now at this time I barely knew R. Kelly. The only thing I knew was he sang, *"You Got That Vibe,"* but I wasn't a big R&B fan (I was more into rap). We pulled up to his condo building on Lakeshore Drive (a valuable piece of real estate). This was where Oprah also had a condo, I was told. When we got to his place all I remember how dirty the place looked, like a real bachelor pad. There was a big 50-inch TV (not a flat screen; this was 1992, so that TV took up a lot of the living room), a black leather couch, a small dining room table and a keyboard, and that was it. I went to the bathroom. Let's just say a maid was needed ASAP. I glanced into his bedroom and spare room, because the doors were cracked open. His bedroom had a big canopy bed in it and clothes everywhere and his spare room had a universal weight set that stretched to the ceiling. Remember, this was before he became the "R." So to me, he was nothing but a dude who sang R&B music that needed a maid.

R, his crew and I decided to get something to eat, so we rolled out to an all-night diner. As we were driving, he let me listen to his new solo album (which would go on to be *12 Play*). He asked me my opinion on song after song (and one thing I did back then, as I do now, was keep it 100% real), so I told him "nah" on some songs and "yes" on others. I remember *"Your Body is Calling"* as being one of the ones I liked. Now in all fairness, he told me they weren't finished or mixed. We went from the diner to a club called the *Clique* (which would be changed to *E2,* where I would almost lose my life years later). I just remember that every place we went to that night, everyone was giving R. Kelly mad props. It was like, *"Hi Mr. Kelly, come on in. Hey Robert, this way to VIP."* I thought, *"All this because of one song?"* Hey, I wasn't thinking about *"Honey Love."*

I don't remember much about that night. But I do remember a few months later, *"12 Play"* came out and he was soon on his way to a level of success many have never seen. He was having hit after hit; it was crazy. All I could think during his rise was *"I was sitting in his Jeep Cherokee having a private listening party."*

The next time I saw him, I was standing in front of *Roscoe's Chicken 'N' Waffles* on Pico Boulevard in L.A. A limo pulled up into the parking lot and R. Kelly rolled down the back window and yelled out, *"what's up?"* He was in town performing on the Soul Train Lady of Soul awards and asked if I'd eat with his entourage. I don't turn down free Roscoe's. It was a good time. But the good times wouldn't last long. Two days later the R. Kelly sex tape broke.

I saw him a few months later in Chicago's Regal Theatre where I was doing a play, *Something She Can Feel* with Charlie Wilson. After the show I was backstage, and R. Kelly came through with his entourage looking for Charlie. When I saw him I said, "Hey R., thanks for coming out." He looked at me and said rudely, "This is my town. I ain't staying in the house." I thought *"hold up motherfucker, I was saying thanks for coming out and supporting the play."* I think he thought I was saying *"good to see you out with that sex scandal looming over your head."* Look, I don't believe in kicking a person that I know while they are down. But if you're gonna come at me foul, then *fuck you.* I have since learned to let things roll off my back.

R. Kelly would go on to beat that case and make more music people love. But I will always know I got a chance to judge his music before he became the "R."

R Kelly-"the night he let me listen to the 12 Play album before anyone else"

Ricky Smiley *(Comic, Actor)*

Ricky was my featured act on the Creative Tour, for ten days in April 1994. I had my cousin, T. Rexx, as our opening act. Talk about us clowning, we had some of the best times because we all could Jone. In every store, mall, club, you name it, we Joned on people. One time I had Ricky in tears and to this day he still reminds me of this. I saw this old lady and she had a bit of an attitude about her. When she walked away I said, "Look at Mary McLeod Bethune with her old Cotton Candy bush ass self" and I started mimicking me eating off the top of her head. And Ricky couldn't stop laughing, I've said much funnier things but that struck a core with him. He would ask me to mimic it again like everyday on the tour.

One time, T. Rexx and I came to Birmingham to perform at a club and Ricky picked us up at the airport and took us to the hotel. He said he'd be back to pick us up for the show but he never showed up. Now that wasn't like the Ricky I know. We didn't hear a word from him, so we found a different ride to club. That night we got some disturbing news. Ricky had been shot that night. Luckily he survived. See, if he had picked us up on time that would have never happened.

A few years later, Ricky and another one of our comic friends, Terry Tuff, came to LA to tape *Comicview.* They didn't have much money for a hotel room so I asked my wife if they could crash on the couch. The night before the taping Ricky was a nervous wreck. I had to talk to him constantly to build his confidence up. It's funny how in control he is now when he does TV, but back then Ricky was a ball of nerves. He went on to have a great set on *Comicview*. I remember he later hosted *Comicview*. And I thought he did a good job.

One time, we did a show in Philadelphia and he was headlining. Now I was HIS feature act. I didn't mind that much because I was getting paid very well. It was an outdoor venue and after I got off, he came on and it started raining. Some people stayed while others left. I didn't get see the 'Ricky Smiley is a star' effect that night. I do remember we were at an after party and he asked me for some advice about child support, because money was starting to come in and he wanted to know what to do.

But I got my 'Ricky is a star' wake up call, when I lived in Dallas in 2001. He was performing at the Bronco Bowl, a place that seats 3,000 plus. I didn't know why he was performing at a place that big. I decided to go to support and thought maybe 500 people would show up, because the 'Ricky Smiley is a star' train hadn't stopped at my stop (I wasn't hating. I just wasn't that up on Ricky). I walked into the Bronco Bowl and the place was packed! I went backstage to talk to Eddie Murphy and Chris Tucker, who I thought were on the show too. But no, just Ricky and a few friends were on the show. When it was time for Ricky to perform, I went into the audience and watched my *"feature act"* take it to the next level. He told jokes, he went off stage and changed into different characters, and in between changes, a movie screen came down and the *Best of Ricky on Comicview* played. He played a piano on stage; the boy put on a great show.

I like Ricky and he's always cool with me. As he became more popular, I heard that he became standoffish to fans (especially if asked to do 'Lil Daryl'). Every time I heard that I was shocked, because I've known Ricky to be a humble, fun-loving guy. Whenever I see him he's always smiling and laughing (I know we have history so maybe I get the best of him) but I hope it's not true what some folks say. To me, Ricky will always be that brother that I hung out with during that tour.

Richard Pryor *(Comic, Actor)*

Around May 1995, I got a phone call from Mitzi Shore (owner of the Comedy Store) saying Richard Pryor was going to do some shows at the club and wanted me to perform in front of him and bring him to the stage. He had a book coming out, *Pryor Convictions*, and was about to embark on a comedy tour. I couldn't believe it! Me, Pierre, a comedian from Maryland, a little blip on the radar of the world of comedy was going to work on the stage with the king of comedy, Richard Pryor!

The night before I was supposed to work with Richard, I tossed and turned and couldn't get any sleep. The next day, the hours didn't pass fast enough. I was so excited to finally get to meet *the* Richard Pryor. That night when I got to the club, I saw that it was packed to capacity with the who's who of the entertainment business. I noticed Richard sitting in the dark next to Mitzi. I was saddened to see that his body was in very bad shape from having Multiple Sclerosis. He was only a shell of his former self. But I couldn't wait to get face to face with a man who changed the comedy game like no other had before him or since.

I walked over to where he was to pay my respects. I bent down to say hello and scared him damn near to death. This was a time when you had to approach him very slowly; any sudden movement would scare him. I thought about how life can be so cruel. One minute you have audiences captivated. The next minute, a disease can have you captivated. I went onstage and introduced him up. He had to be helped by two people to the stage and sat in his chair. It was a very sad moment. His timing was off, but he still had the comedy muscle. He did about thirty minutes. I watched the first night, but the next few nights, I went outside while he performed. I had too much love for him to have this as my last memory of him performing. Something astonishing happened while I was outside chatting with a few comics. Each night, grown men would come outside, crying! I asked them what was wrong and they would say they couldn't handle seeing Richard Pryor that way. They, like me, wanted to remember him in his younger years. This man had a major effect on people's lives.

A week later I got a call from Mitzi, telling me Jennifer, Richard's wife, wanted me to go to Richard's house and help for a *People Magazine* interview. She just wanted me there in case Richard needed help and I was honored to do that. But at the last moment they didn't need me. It was a bit of a let down.

I saw Richard at some awards shows, always being careful to avoid scaring him, and paying my respects. I was sad and happy at the same time when I got the news that he had passed away. Knowing what I knew about him, I don't think Richard would want to have stayed in that condition.

A lot of people liked, loved, or hated Richard Pryor, but the mere fact that people even thought of him was part of his greatness. The reason a lot of comics look up to him is because he gave comics a sense of freedom that burns inside all of us. Many are afraid to release that inner feeling. I will never say I think Richard was nor is the funniest comic that ever lived, or told the best stories I have ever heard or had the best punch lines. But I will say he is *the greatest comic of all time*. He made many comics feel free and willing to take chances like no other comic has. You can't really remember too many comics that came before him, but you sure remember many who came after him. I went and bought his book, and even had him autograph it. I was blown away by the many similarities of our upbringings.

I feel lucky that I got a chance to meet *the* Richard Pryor.

Robert Townsend *(Comic, Actor)*

One night in late 1995 I was performing at the Comedy Act Theatre and when I got off stage, a comic friend of mine came up to me and told me Robert was in the back and had been laughing at me. He was with his female assistant, Charlie, who came over and told me Robert wanted to see me in the back. He told me he was working on something and would have something for me. Here was Robert Townsend, a man who wrote and produced many classic urban movies like *Hollywood Shuffle* and *The Five Heartbeats*, talking to me and only me in a serious conversation. He had me give Charlie my number. I can remember two things about that evening: one, how he kept me in the dark about what the project was, and two, how all the other comics had envy in their eyes. As soon as Robert and Charlie left, a couple of comics started asking me questions about what we discussed. I felt like a King!

I could feel that something was happening with my career. There's a moment in your life when you can feel a shift in your dreams or goals if you really are putting in the work and I could feel something in the air. But I didn't want to get too far ahead of myself (that would come later).

A few weeks later, I got the call to come to the Beverly Hills Hotel to meet Robert and Halle Berry. There I was given the part of David in *B.A.P.S.* I once asked Robert why he took the chance on a first-time actor like me. He said he had a gut feeling about me, but if during rehearsals I wasn't working, he would have replaced me in a hurry. I always came prepared on the set. Robert let me improvise a few times and those moments people really took to (I'll say, if I get a director who will let me breathe as an actor on the set, I'll deliver some jewels).

Working with Robert was great. He really taught me what goes into making a movie, from rehearsing, to coming prepared, to being serious about the art form. I thought he'd be more fun on the set, but he taught me that my first obligation is to what comes on that screen. Everything else is sideline stuff.

As a young, first time actor, I needed to learn the right way first. I know some younger people think he's corny, but let me tell you something; when the lights go off, Robert is just as street as the next guy. He loves edgy humor and he respects "dirty" comics (who are funny). But he made a promise to himself that he wouldn't be known for that. He once told me "Pierre, people may think I'm soft, but who do you think introduced the world to Robin Harris, Damon Wayans, and directed Eddie Murphy in *RAW*. I like edgy comedy. I just won't do it myself." I can respect that.

When I wrote *For Da Love of Money,* he was the first one I asked to read the script. He was kind enough to not only read it, but give me valuable notes.

Years later, around 2005, I was a finalist to be the new host for a late night show on BET and I invited Robert to come see my final live audition. I always feel like I'll get honest feedback from him, even if we disagree at times. I'm the edgy side of Robert. The show never got made; they had a changing of rank at BET, and the new rank didn't want a late night show. But they do now, they have the *Monique show.*

(Side Story)

BET *Comicview* producers once called me in for meeting about possibly being the new host. They asked me how I would make the show better if I were the host. I told them "when I'm the host I'll tell you." You should have seen their faces. Look, my mama didn't raise no fool. I tell you my ideas and then you DON'T hire me and use my ideas, "slightly" modifying them. Not this comic. But like a fool, prior to the meeting (like months earlier) I met with an assistant for one of the head execs at BET and gave her my whole idea for a new and improved *Comicview.* Well a few weeks later, she gave my package back telling me her boss didn't want to look at my package in case we had similar ideas. At that point I realized something had been taken. Needless to say, I didn't get the hosting job. It went to Sheryl Underwood, who did a good job. But there were elements of what I gave to that assistant in that package.

<u>(End of Side Story)</u>

In late 2005 Robert offered me my own show on his new network, The Black Family Channel, after the deal with BET Late Night fell through. But we'd have to film it in Atlanta. He flew me out there and I went to his studio, which was in a converted church. I created my show from A to Z. It was the most work I've ever done. Robert will keep pushing you. He has a way of making you feel like you're not at your best without hurting your feelings.

One night while I was in Atlanta, I finally got a chance to see Robert's "street" side. We were hanging out and we stopped by Diddy's restaurant *Justin's*. Afterwards he was taking me back to his hotel where I had left my car. We pulled up to a light on Peachtree Street and next to us were these two fine young ladies. I started to speak just to mess with them, and they told me they were from New Orleans and Hurricane Katrina had caused them to move to Atlanta. I asked them what they were doing and they said they were going to their apartment, so jokingly I said, "we'll follow you." They started laughing, until Robert leaned over from the driver's side. They got a good look at him and damn near lost their country-ass minds. Then it clicked with them who I was. And they got really excited and said, "cool!!" and sped off. So Robert sped off after them, and followed them through a few streets and freeways at a high ass speed. At first I was thinking *"damn, Robert is a thug ass nicca following these chicks to their crib"* but then I realized how fast they were driving and how fast we were driving and I told him, “fuck them girls, they’re driving way too fast and we don’t need to be chasing these chicks.” Robert finally slowed down and we pulled off the freeway and got lost. I kept looking at Robert thinking, *“This is a real-ass dude.”* Either he was just fucking with me, chasing these girls or I changed his mind from whatever was about to go down. I only told him to stop because my street senses had kicked in and these chicks weren’t really from here. And I didn’t know who they were going to call and tell that we were over their crib.

I like Robert. There wouldn’t be all these young filmmakers if it wasn’t for him and Spike Lee. I am a big admirer of Robert Townsend’s body of work. When you think about the comedians he’s helped discover, from his HBO series *Partners in Crime*, to his TV shows and movies. He is responsible for launching the career of some of our most respected comedians. I don’t think he gets his due respect from the younger generation.

Robert Townsend- in Dallas at a private screening of *10,000 Black Men Named George*

Robin Givens *(Actress)*

It was November 2007, and I was in Oklahoma City rehearsing for a play, *Heaven I Need a Hug.* A week after we began rehearsals, Robin Givens joined the cast. Now I didn't know much about her but what I had heard in the press. This was the woman that had clowned Mike Tyson on national TV. I thought she was a very talented actress. We had a meeting and script read-through with the cast and our "new" cast mate, Robin. The meeting was at 1 p.m., and lunch had been served in the same room at 12:30 p.m. Well I wasn't hungry and knew that we never started on time with rehearsal after lunch. I was tired of being the first person at rehearsals after lunch, sitting around waiting on everyone else to come, so I came in at 1:15 p.m. this time, fifteen minutes past the scheduled start time. As I entered the room, a third of the cast was already there, including Robin. I could feel that something wasn't right. As the rest of the cast, including the writer and one of the leads came in, Robin read us the riot act, about how she "don't need this, she's not use to this unprofessionalism (welcome to most Black plays), and how if we didn't get ourselves together, she was leaving. She had the writer shook. All I could think was, *"Bytch, who do you think you're talking to?"* But in my heart I knew she was right, at least as far as being on time, because we had been slacking off. But her threatening to leave didn't mean shyt to me. I had comedy shows I had canceled to be on this play anyway, so if she's gotta go, then GO. So I told her how I felt about her coming in and telling us how things *should* be, because I felt she was directing her comments at me. As I got in the ass of the whole production, everyone looked at me like *"Damn, you're giving*

Robin Givens, the director, and the writer a piece of your mind!" It was a bit tense in the room when I got through, but that's how I like it; keep it 100% real with me. Get it off your chest, so we know where we stand.

Believe it or not after the read-through, I was asked to walk Robin over to her hotel, which was next to ours. I didn't have any ill feelings towards her, because as I said before, I have a lot of respect for those who speak their minds, even if I don't agree with it. On the walk over, I found her to be pleasant, and easy to talk to. I discovered she was married and had two kids, and she was about to play the role of Wendy Williams in a movie about her life.

Finally, show time came. This was our first show with Robin. It took her about ten minutes to appear on stage for her part, but when she did, I have to be honest: the play went to another level. She was so good and on point! There had been another actress who had done a good job in rehearsals, but nothing like Robin. Robin only did two shows with us and had to go back to Hollywood. By the way, we were never late for rehearsal again. I guess she got her point across.

As I look back, Robin is a classic actress. She's about her work and she's been through so much, she just doesn't have time for anything outside of work. I gained a lot of respect for her in the short amount of time I knew her. Sometimes people's public image is not what they really are behind closed doors.

The Rock *(Actor)*

In 2002 my barber, Rachael, had moved up to the 'Big Time' and was now The Rock's official hair stylist. She asked if I wanted to come on the set of his latest film he was working on, *The Rundown.* Sure, why not? I was excited to meet him, because I had become a fan of his work. You know us light-skinned brothers gotta stick together! When I got to the set, I found Rachael standing by the director. They were in the process of filming the scene where these little jungle fighters catch him in a trap and he was hanging from a tree. I watched for an hour or so and when there was a break in the action, Rachael called the Rock over. He looked like a star—not a hair out of place, skin flawless, and dude was built (no homo). Now he was a pretty big star at the time, but came over and talked to us; no airs, and no macho bullshit that some actors try to pull, he was just cool. We laughed and joked for awhile. I told him I had an idea for a movie for us (he had probably heard that a 1,000 times), but he said to get at him before I left. I thought, *"Yeah right, I've heard that before, but thanks for at least being cool."* After watching another hour or so of filming, it was time to wrap up production. I went to Rachael, thanked her for inviting me to come down and was ready to leave. She told me to go to The Rock's trailer and talk to him about the movie idea, saying he was really cool. I thought, *"What the heck, it can't hurt."* So I went to his trailer and stood by the door, which was open. I could see he was talking to someone, but he saw me standing there and told the person to hold on and came out to talk to me. He gave me his number and told me to call him. I called a few weeks later and left a message, but I never got a return call. But I wasn't mad. He was cool enough to even take time to kick it with me. I know entertainers who are nowhere near his level who wouldn't take a second to speak. From that day on, I became a huge fan of the Rock. You have to admit, he has a personality that you don't expect from a man of that size. I like his comedic timing and his ability to not take himself too seriously. So The Rock is all good in my book. Hopefully one day we'll work together.

Ruben Studdard *(Singer)*

I was performing in the play *Heaven I Need a Hug* and heard that Ruben Studdard would be joining the cast. We had already started rehearsing. It's usually best to be there in the beginning of a play because people start making alliances and building friendships early on. And since there's so much diva-ness going on, you want to pair yourself with someone that you can ride along with for the duration of the play, which can easily stretch out for many months.

I was coming back from eating one day and as I walked in the lobby I saw Ruben and a friend checking in at the counter. So I approached to welcome him and introduce myself (as you should know about me, I will usually make the first approach, but if you're on some bull, then *Fuck You).* Ruben was very cordial. I had a good feeling about him.

During rehearsals he was very open to directions. Sometimes when people first start tasting fame, they have an image they want to present to the public, and they rebuff any ideas that don't fit in. See, people don't realize many times I watched people and their movements; I study people from afar. Sometimes people think I'm being standoffish but I'm just lying back watching, even when you think I'm not.

Ruben's job in the play was to come out, sing a song, say a few lines, then walk off. And at the finale, come back out and sing another song as the curtain falls, and pick up a nice sized check for it. Damn, work is good when you can get it. Many nights Ruben would chill in the lobby and talk with a few of us. He told me the story of when he won *American Idol.* He said that night all of Birmingham, Alabama, was shut down. All I could think was how cool it would be if you have a whole city waiting for one moment, and the moment was for you!

I was pleasantly surprised by how down to earth he was. He cursed and talked trash. It felt like I was sitting with one of my homeboys.

The play only lasted for few more shows. The promoter ran out of money. That's the story with many urban plays.

But Ruben was a cool dude. I hope to see him doing big things.

Russell Simmons *(Mogul)*

It was 1991 and I was in New York City to tape *Def Comedy Jam.* All of the comics from the show were called to the Academy Theatre for a meeting. Russell Simmons came and said a quick "hi." I didn't really get to speak to him much during the taping, but I would watch him every time I saw him come around. There's something about him that grabs your attention. It might be the fact that he was a very successful business man and he dressed like he was hanging on the street corner. He interacted with everyone like he was one of them.

The next time I would actually speak to him was in 1996 when I came in to audition for *How to Be a Player* (he was one of the executive producers). As soon as I walked in he said, *"This is a funny nigga."* This was in front of five other casting directors and producers, so I was a little taken aback; not because he called me a funny nigga, but because of his freedom to curse in front of people. True, he knew all of them, but this was a professional audition. But that's Russell, he says and does what he feels. I wasn't offended. In fact I took it with a sense of pride. I got the part.

Russell saw me at a party in Hollywood a few years later and told me (he doesn't really ask), "I got a new TV show, One World Music Beat (it was like a hip-hop version of Entertainment Tonight), and you're gonna host the news segment. You ain't scared to do it right? And I'm paying you $1,000 a show and I don't want to talk to no manager or agent." Then he gave me his address and told me to go to his house the next day and pick up some clothes made by his label,

Phat Farm, which he wanted me to wear on the show. Wow, this man didn't know me well at all and he trusted me to go to his house by myself. I wouldn't trust a motherfucker to look around in my car! On my way to his house, all I could think was how cool he was to do that.

I drove up to his home in the Hollywood Hills. I pulled in on a slanted hill (hello, they call it Hollywood Hills for a reason) and put in the security code for the gate. As I entered his home and saw how nice it was, I was surprised that he kept his front door unlocked. His house wasn't huge, but very stylish. If my memory serves me correctly he had a koi pond. As I entered his home I noticed it was set up like a slick bachelor pad. You could tell he traveled the world by the things that were in his home. What struck me was all of the boxes of clothes that were scattered all over the place. He had told me that the clothes I would be picking up were in his bedroom. As I got to his bedroom, I saw an unkempt contemporary bed and Phat Farm clothes everywhere, a few pairs of Adidas, and not a pair of dress shoes in sight. By the looks of things, you could tell he was always on the go. I didn't go snooping around. I take pride in people's trust and felt no desire to go snooping. I grabbed the clothes I came for and was off. I ended up working on his show for about a year, until I had to go to Europe to film a movie.

Russell also let me get $1,000 worth of Phat Farm gear from his New York City boutique whenever I was in town. I still have some of those clothes to this day. Hey, they were well made.

Once while I was living in Phoenix in 2006, Russell came to town to promote something at a club, so I went there to see him. When I got there, I noticed a crowd had gathered around him and there were security guards around holding people at bay. I approached, and of course one of the bodyguards was taking his job way too seriously (memo to overzealous security guards: *Chill!!*) and held me back. Russell saw me and looked me in the eye, then looked away and back to the girl who was in his face. I thought, *"Hold up, hold up! Did this nicca just play me? Motherfucker, I was in your house and could have done you wrong."* I stood there for a second, trying to make sense of the moment, and trying to convince myself that he didn't see me. Then I thought, *"Fuck that, he saw me. I was only three feet away from him!"* Just as I was going to walk away, Russell signaled to one of his goons to let me through and spoke to me briefly. But by that time, I felt differently about him. I'm still a huge fan of Russell. Anyone who starts from humble beginnings and doesn't conform to typical business methods and becomes hugely successful, I take my hat off to them.

Shaq *(Basketball player)*

I was walking down the Sunset Strip one afternoon and walked past this little clothing boutique, and noticed something way too big moving around inside there. So I stopped and took a few steps back and saw that lo and behold, BIG-ass Shaq was in there with his homeboy who is always sitting behind him at games. It looked like a tyrannosaurus rex was trying to make a call in a phone booth. I greeted him and he grabbed my hand to shake it, and next thing I knew my hand was gone. He told me he thought I was funny, and I told him I was funny because I practiced, like he should do with his free throws. He just laughed it off, but I was serious.

In the summer of 2002, I was in San Antonio doing a show and the Lakers were there playing the Spurs in the conference finals. I went to a club after my show and when I got there, I saw half of the Lakers (except Kobe) in there dancing with all the best females San Antonio had to offer. All I could think was damn, first you beat the shit out of the Spurs, now you're in here dancing with their women. Damn, life must be *good.* I noticed Shaq in VIP, so I walked over to him. He offered me anything I wanted in VIP, so I pointed at a female and said, "I'll take one of those!" (Just kidding.) You never realize how big Shaq is until you see him standing next to other basketball players, and he's *bigger* than them! I spoke with Shaq for a moment and went on about my way.

When I was living in Phoenix, I would occasionally run into him at parties. He'd always be surprised to see me in the house. We felt like we kept popping up at the same spots. Everyone loves to be in his presence. You'll never see Shaq standing by himself. I've seen some big stars give off a standoffish vibe, but not him. I think he likes having people all around him. I have a feeling Shaq and I will be running into each other soon.

Shemar Moore *(Actor)*

In the summer of 1999, I first met Shemar at one of Jamie Foxx's parties. This party was in the Hills, about an hour outside of LA. There was nothing but White people in that area, and Jamie had like 300 Black folks partying poolside, on the tennis courts, around the house—everywhere but IN the house. Jamie was hot at the time, with his show, *The Jamie Foxx Show*, so a lot of young Hollywood came out. I never paid Shemar any attention before. As far as I was concerned, he was just a pretty boy soap actor. At the party he had the usual females around him, wanting pictures and autographs. I could tell he's one of those 'sit back and watch' kind of guys. I asked for a picture to add to my collection. He is definitely into "Shemar Moore" and what "Shemar Moore" represents. He knows he's sexy, so he's got to stand right, wear sexy shirts, and sexy jewelry. I can't be mad at him. If it's paying the bills, then cash in on it. He doesn't come off as an asshole, just someone who is really focused on being who he is, and knowing his brand.

The next time I ran into him, we both were entering a restaurant in Hollywood. When I saw him, I was taken aback by what he was wearing. He had on some karate looking shoes, with Hammer pants (well, that's what they looked like) and a tight shirt. I asked him, "Were they casting for the *Last Dragon 2?*" I never realized his bottom teeth were jacked up. Don't get me wrong, my bottom row ain't perfect, but at this time he had the money and was all about his looks, so I was a bit surprised. I heard he's since got them shyts straightened out. Good look. We sat down and had a quick conversation, and to be real with ya'll he's a real down to earth dude. Not what I expected. He's just one of those dudes who is really focused, and in this business that's what you have to be.

We parted ways and I haven't seen him since, but he's doing his thing on *Criminal Minds*.

Shemar Moore- at Jamie Foxx's summer party

Sherri Shepherd *(Comic, Actress)*

Sherri and I came up together around the comedy club scene early in the 90's. She wouldn't perform at all the places I would (I didn't care where a stage was, just give me the mic). She performed at more respectable spots. Sherri was more personality than humor. She had the "sista" thing down, a lot like she is on *The View*.

Sherri and I had a little sexual chemistry between us; nothing we acted upon, but it was there. Whenever we saw each other, we would comment on what we might do to each other if it got further. I always thought she was just a cool female comedian. So many female comedians aren't happy because they are not in loving relationships. Many men don't want women who are on stage talking shit about them or doing sexually explicit material. Unless she's rich and famous, then a man will deal with it. But if she isn't, most men won't go there. And that's why female comics feel left out many times. They try to act or be a way they really aren't, which in turn makes male comics treat them unfairly. Sherri never came off like she was trying too hard to fit in, at least not to me.

I was surprised one night when Sherri called just to chit chat; usually we'd only talk at the clubs. She said she wanted to come over. The only catch was I'd have to pick her up. She lived in or near Koreatown, a little shadier area than what I was expecting Sherri to live in. At the time, I was living in a studio apartment in LA. I picked her up, and brought her back to my place. We watched a little TV, and talked about the business and how fond of each other we were. She struck me as a good girl, so I wasn't trying to put the moves on her. But before I knew it one thing led to another and this would be the night we would put up or shut up.

We pulled out my futon and stripped down to our underwear, and the moment got hot and heavy. Well folks, you know when a man gets hot and heavy, things expand and lengthen (did I tell you I was half Black?). Let just say she didn't want to attempt that feat. And quickly changed her mind. To be honest, I wasn't even mad. I've never been the "I'ma take it" kind of guy, so we stopped. But she was still tripping about what she saw. She said she was surprised and in disbelief (pretty much like you are right now...). We got dressed and I drove her back home and gave her a hug. It truly wasn't a big deal to me that we didn't go through with it; not to say I didn't want to.

The next evening Sherri called me and once again asked me to pick her up and bring her back to my apartment. I was in the middle of cooking some dinner, but I put it on hold. Now I was getting excited, thinking she finally thought it over and wanted to go through with it. I picked her up and we talked and laughed about the business as we drove back to my place, telling stories about how we were going to make it and why. We got to my apartment, and I finished making dinner (ladies, ya boy likes to cook). We watched a little TV and we started in on kissing. Now I was getting really hot, and stretched out as far as my body parts could go because I was anticipating getting some. She grabbed it and stopped; she apologized and said she couldn't do it. I was thinking, *"Girl it didn't get no smaller in 24 hours."* Now I was a little pissed, and told her we had to leave. All I thought was "*I drove all the way to get you, brought you to my house, gotta take you all the way back and then come all the way back home for nothing?*" We didn't do any talking on the drive home. I saw her a few times after that. Our careers started taking off. She was working on sitcoms and I was doing movies. But after that night, I didn't have any hard feelings for her. I know she didn't mean any harm, and I never thought she was trying to play me. She's too sweet of a woman to do that.

Now when I see her on *The View*, I'm happy for her. The same bubbly, intelligent woman you see now, I saw in 1991. I have never told anyone this story, and the only reason I told it now is because she has come out and told similar stories about herself and how she *used to* be. Hey, when you're young, you do things and we all were young once.

Sinbad *(Comic, Actor)*

In the early 90's, Sinbad's brother Mark, who managed him, was interested in managing me also. But we couldn't make it happen. I really didn't think I would be a good fit, out of respect for Sinbad and his clean image. I didn't want to change who I was to be under the "Sinbad" umbrella, even though I had a lot of respect for him.

I had seen Sinbad around many times, but had never spoken to him. I ran into him at the Baldwin Hills Crenshaw Plaza while I was doing some promotions for a radio station. We just said our "hellos." But I really got to hang out with him in Arizona in 2006. When I heard he was coming to a local theatre, I called up Mark and got two tickets to the show. I was excited to see him, because I had never seen him live before. When I got to the 3,000-seat theatre, I was a little surprised it wasn't sold out. This was a brand new theatre complex. The place was less than a third filled, and many were White folks. But, this was Arizona. I was happy to see any Black folks.

We found our seats, which were very good, and sat down. Now Sinbad had music playing before coming out, but what struck me as odd was that he had rap playing. He had Ludacris' *"Move Bitch"* playing (the dirty version). Yes, *"Move bitch, get out the way, move bitch..."* I had to look around to make sure I was at the right show. He didn't have an opening act, which I thought was strange. He just walked out on stage and started performing. Sinbad had a good show. It seemed like he was working on his act. Halfway through his act, he started asking the audience to yell out subjects they wanted him to talk about. Damn, that's bold. But he was ready. Everything they threw at him, he threw back with humor. That takes talent!

My girlfriend and I went backstage to meet him after the show. He was very jovial. He invited us to have sushi with him and a few friends. Let me tell you, Sinbad is a crazy street dude. At dinner, he talked about everything he couldn't on stage. And to hear him curse was a trip. We talked about his daughter who went to college there. He told me something fascinating. He believed he would have made more money as a comedian if he had been edgier. I was pleasantly surprised at how fun Sinbad was.

A few years later I heard on the news that he had died, but later found out it was just a hoax. I haven't run into him since that concert, but I know when I do, we'll trip.

Sinbad on the set of *The VIBE TV Show*

Snoop *(Rapper, Actor)*

Snoop and I didn't officially meet until years after I had been in L.A. That's kind of surprising because we knew a lot of the same people. I met him in August 2004 on the set of the video *Groupie Luv* that he and Warren G were shooting. It was directed by my good friend, Chris Robinson. He called me one day and asked if I would like to do a cameo in the video as a favor. And because Chris is good people, I was down. I usually don't do anything that makes money for free.

I had to drive really far to the outskirts of L.A. way up in the hills. I got to the set, signed a few papers and then wardrobe called me over and gave me an outfit. I saw Chris. He told me what he needed me to do and said he'd call me back on set when he was ready for me. I told him since I was doing this as a favor, I only had a two hour window to work with because of a previous engagement. He was cool with that and said that was plenty of time. I started walking around meeting some of the behind-the-scenes people, and making idle conversation. I walked down to the set to watch a little bit of the filming. Snoop and Warren G were on a tennis court. I don't remember much of the video, except that there were some fine ass women walking around. I noticed a couple of them were female porn starts. Rappers always do videos right, with great eye candy. If you ever wanna see some honeys, go to a rap video set. Now the chances are slim that you would find your wife there, unless she was working production.

After about an hour, I got called over to Snoop's trailer. I was told he wanted to meet me. As I approached his trailer, I could smell the aroma of the finest California sticky-icky (and we ain't talking about taffy). As I entered, he was there surrounded by his crew. He has such a laidback demeanor. Snoop, barely able to open his eyes, smiled at me and said, "You's a funny motherfucker." He asked me if I wanted to join into a smokefest. I told him I would have to pass on that. After that he was called back to the set. How that boy could function in that condition is still a mystery to me. But he is truly one of the coolest rappers in the game, and I would work with him anytime.

Snoop- backstage at Master P's Comedy All Star in LA

Steve Harvey *(Comic, Actor)*

I first met Steve when he brought me to his comedy club *Vu Cu Rea's* in Dallas. He was the house MC and ran the club. I was fresh off of *Def Comedy Jam* and he brought me there to headline (that means you do at least forty-five minutes on stage). Now at this point in my career, I barely had that much material, but he was paying me $800 for the week, and back in 1992 that was a whole lot of money. Hell, my rent was only $475 a month, so I took it. The first night, Steve opened the show with twenty of the funniest minutes of comedy this crowd had ever heard, and then brought up the feature act. After that Steve went back up and did another twenty minutes, even funnier than his first twenty minutes. I was looking out of the dressing room thinking there was a damn riot going on, people falling out of their chairs, glass breaking, people high-fiving each other. Every time I closed and opened the door again, it seemed there was more commotion. I thought a fire had broken out and the fire marshal had come in! Well, I was wishing they would so they could stop the show because I did not want to follow that shyt.

Well, it was time for me to go on stage. Steve called my name and handed me the mic, and gave me a look like Michael Jordan used to give Spike Lee after an amazing shot before he would run back up the court. As I stood in the center of the stage, it was as if the crowd just stared at me. It was as if I was looking at a photo of the audience—just still. They looked at me like, "*Ok, what do you have to say?*" I started my act and got a few chuckles, courtesy laughs and smiles. I had an OK set. I had just had my comedy ass handed to me by a true professional. The next show that night went the same way. The next day, Steve called me to the side before the show and told me I only had to do fifteen minutes of material this time. Now I don't know if this was from the kindness of his heart, because he didn't want to see a young comic struggle, or because he wanted to keep the show at a certain level for the audience. Whatever the reason, I appreciated it. When the week was over and it was time to get paid, I just knew he was going to deduct my pay. But he wrote me a check for the full amount and thanked me for coming. Steve is a class act. He ended up moving to a new location a few years later, and brought me back to perform. By then I was ready, and wanted to show him how much I had improved. But he was out of town that week.

He taught me a few lessons in the comedy game. Between performances at his clubs in 1994, we were booked for a show at the Tampa Performing Arts Center, a place that holds 3,000 people. Only 300 showed up. Of course this was way before Steve would become one of the *Kings of Comedy*. I went on before him and was down because no one showed up. I went out there and bullshitted, talked about the audience and gave a poor performance. What did I care? There wasn't anyone out there anyway! After I left the stage, I passed a waiting Steve, and looked at him like, *"Come on, let's get this over with and go to a club."* Steve went out there and tore the house down. He performed like it was packed in there. I watched this unfold from the side of the stage, and it clicked. As a comic, you go out there and perform for those people who paid to see you. It's not *their* fault the place is empty; they did their part and showed up. I never gave another half-ass performance again. Ask anyone who has ever come to a show of mine. I will give you a show even if it's just you and I. You paid for a great show, and I owe you that.

That night I went up to Steve's hotel room after the show and it was just the two of us. I remember he had his suit laid out on the chair, I mean like *"the first day of school"* laid out. He was sitting in the other chair so I had to sit on his bed. It was as if his suit had its own seat and I had to find somewhere else to sit. But that night, he schooled this young comic on the ways of the game. I will always be thankful for that. I have heard many times that Steve is arrogant, Steve is stuck up, Steve is this and that. I know Steve has a heart. Sometimes you have to walk in someone's shoes, now that is not an excuse to act a fool, but it may help to forgive a person. I've been around him when the lights were dim. I know some of where he came from. Over the years I would see him in passing, and he always took time to sit and speak with me. I always wanted to work with him again, to show him what I learned, but it hasn't worked out. Steve Harvey would go on to mega-success with his TV shows, concerts, radio show and books. Now when I see the "Big Steve Harvey," I chuckle when I think back and remember the time when only 300 people showed up to see him. I'll always be thankful for the knowledge he kicked my way.

Tank *(Singer)*

I was hosting the *Budweiser Super Fest Tour* in August 1997 and Tank was touring with us as a backup singer for Aaliyah and Ginuwine. I would see him onstage and backstage, but I didn't meet him until one day when we were playing at the Nutter Center in Dayton, Ohio. We ran into each other in the hotel laundry room. He had a really cool demeanor. We found out that we grew up very close to each other and knew some of the same people. We clicked really quickly, and would hang out at the malls in some of the different cities. To be honest, I didn't think of him as a future star. He was too shy, and very humble; and didn't exude star quality. Plus he was in the background.

Years later I was watching BET one day, and the next thing I knew the *"I Deserve"* video aired. I was like, "that's Tank!" I understand the feeling my old friends get when people say they like me or get excited about me. Because when Tank started blowing up, I thought about how I could remember knowing him when no one else knew him. When girls started going crazy over him, I'd laugh inside and just listen to them. I later found out he had become a heck of a producer and songwriter. He has written and produced many hits for Jamie Foxx among others. We would run into each other at Hollywood parties and always laugh at how far we've come. He had the coolest manager, Muhammad. He was always working on something for Tank, and always wanted to put me down with some project.

A few years ago I was doing a show in Fayetteville, North Carolina, and I heard he was in town performing at a club. After my set, my road managers and I went to catch his show. As soon as he saw me, a big smile crossed his face. We embraced each other like old friends. He took the stage and all the ladies rushed the stage and all the fellas fell back with a bit of jealousy.

Every once in a while when I'm traveling I'll run into him at the airport. We're always going somewhere. One day it would be cool to do a tour together "The Love 'n' Laughter Tour."

Tasha Smith *(Actress)*

It was 1995, and I was a rising comic. I had done a few TV comedy shows. There was a mini-comedy tour, where you played nightclubs and comedy clubs. It was put together by the *Comedy Zone* comedy club chain, and was ten shows, in ten days, in seven cities. It started in Norfolk, Virginia, and went through the southern states, ending up in Macon, Georgia. The deal with the tour was that the "*headliner*" got to choose a feature act, but that feature act had to drive the headliner from city to city. If the headliner couldn't find a feature to do that, the club would provide a local comic who would be willing to do the driving.

Tasha had heard I was doing the tour and called to ask if she could feature for me. Now I'd seen Tasha in passing at comedy clubs around LA, and I had spoken with her a few times before. I wouldn't say we were good friends, but I thought she was cool. She had raw talent but I dug her personality. Tasha was funny, but very vulgar and very descriptive, almost like one of the fellas. So I said yes, but I told her the deal: that she would have to drive. She was cool with that and said she'd fly there and rent a car and drive us.

We performed at the first *Comedy Zone* stop in Virginia. It was for three nights. After the second night, the owner's father Gabe, who ran the club, said he did not like her act or her vulgarity and told me he was going to call his son, Brad (the owner in North Carolina) and have her taken off the tour. I begged him not to, but he wasn't hearing it. I told him I'd talk to her and that he should give her one more chance the next night. Why I did this, I don't know. I could have easily said *"fuck her,"* but I guess I was there once myself. After talking to him again, he agreed and I went to her and explained the situation. She wasn't happy, but agreed to tone down her show the next (and last) night. Despite all of that, the remainder of the shows went well. We got paid and I embarked upon what was about to be the journey from Hell.

The next morning, we had packed her rental car and were about to pull off for our four hour drive to the next city for that night's show. She asked me to drive because she didn't feel well. I thought, *"Hold up, the purpose of them pairing up a feature act for the trip was so the headliner wouldn't be tired."* And I hadn't wrapped my mind around driving at all. Hell, I knew other comics who would have killed to be on the road working. Just the year before, I had Ricky Smiley driving for me! So I told her no, plus I hadn't brought my license. She BLEW up with anger, called me all types of names, slammed doors. I wish she had been a man; she would have gotten knocked out. I got in the passenger seat and we drove off, with her still pissed. She had the new CD by Meshell N'Degeocello and she blasted the CD for four hours, over and over. When I say blasted, I mean *blasted!* (I would later meet Meshell who's a sweetheart), but by then I wanted no parts of her or the fact that *"if that's your boyfriend he wasn't last night"* song. All I could think now was, *"You ungrateful bytch. I saved yo ass so you could stay on this tour and this is how you're gonna act?"*

We got to the next city, didn't speak one word before or after the show, and drove on to our next city. I was actually cool with that, because by that time I had grown to dislike her and the less she said, the better off I was. Well, we pulled into the hotel in Raleigh, North Carolina and she informed me that she wasn't driving me to the next city, which was Charlotte (the halfway point of the tour and where Brad lived and ran our next club). I got to my room and called the booking agent, Nate, to inform him of what she had said. He told me to knock on her door and ask her to come to the phone. I told him I didn't want to but for the good of everyone else, I would. I went across the hall and knocked on her door, still holding the phone with

Nate on the line. She yelled through the door, *"Motherfucker, get the fuck away from my goddamn door, motherfucker!"* Even Nate heard it through the phone. He asked me to catch a bus to Charlotte the next day, which was about a two hour ride. I did the show that night, and the next day I got on the bus and went to Charlotte. All I could think was, *"How in the world am I the headliner, picked my feature act and wind up on the bus?"* The things you guys don't know about.

In Charlotte, after Tasha performed, the owner kicked her off the tour, and that was her last show with me. I went on to the next cities without her and with a new feature. I heard she and her manager had threatened to sue the club. Really?

I saw her a few more times right after that around L.A. I even met her identical twin sister, Sidra. When I say identical, I mean even their gynecologist couldn't tell them apart. (lol) The only way to identify them was if you went by personality. Sidra was so sweet, very soft spoken and kind. Tasha was brash, loud and vulgar. Even Sidra knew this and she would approach people with, "Hi, I'm NOT Tasha, I'm her sister Sidra." Can you imagine having to do that every time you met someone for the first time? Sidra and I became cool. But whenever I saw her I would be hesitant when I approached her. She'd look at me and say, "Pierre, it's Sidra."

Years passed and I hadn't seen or heard from Tasha. Then one day I ran into her and she apologized for that trip. She said she was born again and told me she was a changed person and would I forgive her. After that her and I were cool. I have a lot of respect for those who can admit when they're wrong. Tasha has gone on to fame, starring in Tyler Perry movies, and has become a very sought after acting coach and teacher. I'm truly happy to see how far she has come.

Tavis Smiley *(Talk show host)*

The only time I ever met Tavis was while I was promoting *For Da Love of Money* in 2002. I went to his studio in LA. I really didn't know much about him. I was a little surprised to see that he had a studio in the hood. I was doing so many interviews at that time, and thought this would be just another one. This interview was on his radio show, heard on National Public Radio. I was introduced to him and he was a man of big stature, and had a big smile on his face. His assistant took me into this little room with just enough space for him and I, and we proceeded to do the interview. I found him to be really engaging and funny, but best of all, he laughed at EVERYTHING I said. I swear I couldn't go wrong. I thought, *"I gotta take this guy on the road with me and put him in the front row of all my shows."* I'd have to say this is my favorite interview of all time that I have ever done. He made me feel like he actually cared about what I had to say and asked some great questions. I don't know how long we were on air but it felt like it wasn't enough time.

After that, I started watching his show on PBS and now I see how an interview is supposed to be done. The boy is good. I wish more people would watch his show. I guess people would rather watch some bullshyt reality show, than watch a Black man engaging in intelligent conversation. That's a shame. Hopefully one day I can do his show. In the past few years, Tavis has gotten himself into and out of hot water. He likes to touch the hot buttons that affect the Black community. Tavis can interview me anytime.

Terrence Howard *(Actor)*

In 1998, I was on Sunset Boulevard one afternoon at an outdoor music and arts and crafts festival in West Hollywood. I was enjoying the music when I saw this guy dressed up, looking like Jimi Hendrix with a guitar slung over his shoulder. My first thought was, *"ain't yo ass supposed to be on stage?"* Then I noticed it was Terrence. Now we had never officially met, but we had gone up against each other for movie parts. He spoke, and said he was auditioning for the *Jimi Hendrix Story.* What I also noticed, besides his outfit, was the way he spoke. It was like he was out of the 60's or 70's. We parted ways, and all I could think about was how he was a bit odd. But I respected the fact that he took his craft so seriously that even though he didn't have the part yet, he was in character now.

I ran into him many years later in July 2006 while we were backstage at the Essence Festival in Houston. I was there with my daughter and he was there with his young daughter. He said his daughter wanted to take a picture with me because I was in one of her favorite movies, *B.A.P.S.* How crazy because her father almost had that part. I took the picture with pleasure and got a picture with him and my daughter to add to her collection.

Terrence has a career that I envy. He is constantly working and puts out very good performances. He is one of the actors that I admire. If I were to lose out to a part to him, I could accept that. A lot of people want to label him as just a "pretty boy" but you have to give credit where credit is due he's one of the best young actors out there. I have major respect for him as an actor. *(See photo)*

Three 6 Mafia *(Rap group)*

It was the spring of 2000. My wife and I had just separated and I was feeling great with the newfound space. I felt like I finally had the freedom to pursue my career the way I needed to. And if I could make things right in my career, maybe my wife and I could work things out. I got a call from a video producer telling me that the rap group Three 6 Mafia wanted me to appear in Project Pat's new video *"Don't Save Her."* Now I didn't know who he was and all I had heard about T6M was that their songs invoked a lot of fighting in clubs. *"Tear da club Up."*

I requested my usual fee and told them they had to fly my "road manager" Joe P., with me for the two day shoot. To my surprise they were good with that. Rap videos usually have limited budgets and try to cut back on extras. We got to Miami the night before the shoot, checked into the hotel and ran around the city like two kids, looking for something to get into. The next morning we got to the set, which was on the beach, and met Gil Green, the young director. I thought it was strange that a young White guy was directing this video. I had always seen Black guys directing hip-hop videos up until this point. After talking with him, I could see why they chose him. He had the smarts, and knowledge of what hip-hop audiences wanted at the time: funny and sexy. I got the storyline and found out what they needed me to do.

They had gathered some of the sexiest young ladies you'd ever wanted to see to be in this video. A few minutes later T6M came onto the beach. They were a bunch of fun loving guys, more like some frat guys than the bunch of thugs that I thought they were. When it came time to shoot the video, I was informed that Project Pat wouldn't actually be in the video because he was in jail. I didn't know who the hell Project Pat was so when they had a stand in, I didn't even know he was the stand in. He had to be shot from the back so that the viewers wouldn't know he wasn't the real Project Pat.

Gil gave me the freedom to be funny, which I took full advantage of. We had a really good rapport. During breaks in the filming, I sat in a trailer and met one of their other artists, Gangsta Boo. She was really cool, but no matter how "gangsta" a woman artist is, a video shoot full of guys is no place for a woman if she doesn't have any female friends around. I felt like she was uncomfortable. Either that or she was just bored with sitting around.

Now the dude with the most personality on the set and who could damn near give me a run for my money when it came to Jonin' was Crunchy Black. I've never seen a person that dark in America. He could touch charcoal and leave fingerprints. When I first met him, I thought he was my shadow. I was wondering why my shadow wasn't moving when I moved! He had to learn how to Jone damn near at birth, because you know how kids are. But he was a good dude about the way I was killin' him. Juicy and Paul loved every minute of it. They were just trying to keep me off of their asses. I had a great time all around making that video. When it came out, I got a lot of love from down south. Everywhere I went people were asking me about Project Pat. They wanted jail updates, like I served time with him.

The group called me again when they came to LA to do the *"Baby Mama"* video. I went down to the set and they tried to get me in the video, but their pockets were empty and my humor meter was also on 'E'. So I had to pass. I won't say that I will not do something for free, but if you've got that money, I want some. You can't be riding in Rolls Royce's and living in a big house and not throw your boy a few stacks.

The next time I saw Paul and Juicy was June 8, 2002, in Memphis for the Tyson/Lewis fight. I was coming out of the Peabody Hotel and they were riding up in a Rolls Royce convertible (damn, I gotta become a rap producer). We spoke for a minute and said we'd see each other around and that was the last time I've seen them. We all know they went on to win an Oscar and to do that awful reality show (I gotta keep it 100% real. They know it's all love over here). I enjoy the fact that I am friends with one of the biggest groups in the Southern hip-hop movement. They will always be my homeboys.

Hanging with Joe P. and Three 6 Mafia at a video shoot in LA.
Can you guess which one is Crunchy Black?

Tom Joyner *(Radio host)*

In March 2003, I was performing at the Improv Comedy Club in Dallas. The Improv asked if I wanted to do an interview on the *Tom Joyner Morning Show*, even though his show didn't air in Dallas. He was syndicated in over 100 markets, so I thought, *"why not?"* It would be more publicity for future markets. I got in the studio and right off the bat, I felt the love. Myra J., Ms. Dupree, J. Anthony Brown and I go way back. Since Tom and I look somewhat alike (me being a younger, more handsome version, lol), we told everyone I was his long lost son. I was amazed at how easily I fit in with everyone so quickly. Sometimes it can take awhile to get the rhythm in these situations. I had a ball in the studio and was looking forward to working with Tom again. I tried to be a comic on his cruise, but each time someone already working with him thwarted my effort. I don't think it was personal, just bad timing (well, I'll tell myself that) because I was and am just as funny as any of the comics he had on those cruises.

Tom helped me with my house and he doesn't even know it. I had just bought a house in April 2006 and was doing a remodeling job before I moved in. Well the money ran low and I had to decide what I could have done then, and what I would have to wait on (I hate waiting). I got a call from a friend of mine to do a Tuesday night show in Houston at a jazz club for $1,000 plus a few hundred for travel expenses. At this time I was willing to take anything to make money to put towards my house, so I wouldn't have to dip into my savings. So I agreed, but a few minutes later Tom Joyner's people called and asked if I would be interested in doing a Sky Show in Nashville the Wednesday after my Houston show. I asked for the details, and the lady said, “We don’t have much money.” I asked how much they had to offer, thinking it would be one or two grand. She said, “We ONLY have $5,000 with an additional $750 for travel expenses.” After I silently jumped up and down, I coolly said, “I think I might be able to make that work.”

My flight from Phoenix to Houston, to Nashville and back to Phoenix was $331. OK, kids, let’s do the math: $5,000 + $750 + $1,000 + $300 = $7,750 - $331 (flight) = $7,419 for a Tuesday and Wednesday of work. Works for me!! I mean, you guys might be ballin’ and that might be nothing to you. But let’s just say I got hardwood floors and French doors leading out to my pool, and a TV built into my living room wall. Thanks, Tom!

Tommy Davidson *(Comic, Actor)*

I had just started in the comedy game around 1987 and every once in a while I would hear about a very funny Black comic named Tommy Davidson. Now, he never performed at any of the White comedy clubs or spots. Instead he was always the opener for nationally known musical groups that would come through town at big venues. I never went to any of those shows so I never saw him. I just heard about him as if he were "Bigfoot." Something you hear about, but never see.

A year into my comedy career I was asked to enter a local talent contest, which was the biggest in the city. I swept through the first two rounds and made it to the finals. The finals were held at a 2,200-seat theatre. I heard Tommy had gotten to the finals also. So the night of the finals came, and in the comedy category there were six comics. I met Tommy backstage, and to be honest, I wasn't impressed. He was skinny, and looked like he had just come in off the streets. Everyone else was dressed up but he had on some high-top tennis shoes, some baggy workout pants and a colorful t-shirt (I was thinking, *"look at this clown"*). I had my brand new suit from *Merry Go Round* on, with my patent leather shoes (Oh, if you're over thirty-five, don't act like you didn't have a pair of patent leather shoes). What I did notice was how jovial this nicca was. As if he knew he was going to win. Most young entertainers get really quiet before a performance. Not Tommy, he acted as if it were no big deal.

Well, I was the second comic to go up and didn't do well. I learned a valuable lesson that night that has been with me ever since.

My "friends" told me I would probably be funnier if I was high, so I had gone out behind the theatre and inhaled some of D.C.'s best smoke and drank some vodka. I was trying to win this shit, hell, Richard Pryor got high a lot, and look how well he did. I was only twenty years old and had never drank or smoked before. By the time my name was announced, your boy was feeling right (smile), but not right for a damn comedy show. I remember during my act repeating a joke. I remember people who came to cheer me on in the front row, looking at me like, *"this is not the Pierre we came to see,"* and all I could do was give them a *cannabis* smile. I felt like I had an out-of-body experience, like I was standing next to myself saying *"what the hell are you doing?"* I finished my set without the thunderous applause I was used to in that competition. I instantly knew I had blown it. From that day on I told myself I would never use any substance to enhance my performance.

When it was time for Tommy to perform, I went out in the audience to see what people's reactions would be. The minute, no, the *second* Tommy hit the stage, he had them. I mean, this dude was full of energy, doing impressions, voices, singing his Black interpretation of the national anthem; you name it, he could do it. I had never seen someone with all those weapons live before. I knew then, not only did I see the winner that night, but a future star.

I met my future manager, Ron, there that night. He was working with Tommy. He would later tell me that he approached me that night because he saw something in me, even "high" on stage. Really?

Tommy was off to Hollywood very shortly after that. Soon he was shooting the pilot (first episode) of *In Living Color* and invited Ron (he wasn't managing Tommy anymore, he was now handling me) and I to come out to L.A. and watch the taping. We had a ball watching him shine at the taping. I moved to LA a year later and would run into Tommy from time to time, and he'd *always* show me D.C. love. I later heard that after *In Living Color*, Tommy hit an all time low with drugs. I was sad for him, because Tommy is a good person (amongst many ugly people). A few years after that he pulled himself together and got back to doing what he does best: making people laugh.

I had the pleasure of finally working on the same concerts with him several times in the past few years and this time it wasn't 1987. I brought the show! He was still funny (Tommy is always going to be Tommy), but I had to prove to myself and him that I had grown, even though I knew I had. Hell, it had been twenty years! You know how it is when someone affected you in high school and now you see them at the class reunion. You want them to know you ain't the same person they knew, even if they don't remember you.

Tommy invited me to his house for Thanksgiving in the Hollywood Hills in 2006, and as I always say, I was proud to see how far he had come. To see family around him was a good look for him. He loves to have D.C. people around him. I believe he's a little hurt that Martin Lawrence has never really embraced the DC comedians like he imagined or wished he would have. I myself, sometimes wish us D.C. comics would have come together for a show, special or tour. Think of it: Dave Chappelle, Martin Lawrence, Tommy, Wanda Sykes, Monique, Chris Thomas (BET Rap City Mayor), Joe Clair, Earthquake, a few more and me. I look at it like this: Martin doesn't owe anyone anything, but it would have been a hot tour.

Tommy and I would always talk about doing a project together. I would love that. I think we would act like complete fools. If you see Tommy on the road performing, go out and support him.

Tupac *(Rapper, Actor)*

Around May 1996, I got a phone call from a casting director saying Tupac himself wanted me to be in his video for the song, *"All About You."* I thought, *"Yeah right, he just got out of jail, and it's not like he knows me."* She asked me how much I would charge to shoot for his video for two days. Now I had heard people say they made between $75 and $150 per day to be in a video. So not believing the offer was true, I said $800 per day. There happened to be this bracelet I wanted to buy for that exact amount that I had seen in the mall earlier that day. She told me she would get back with me and hung up. So I thought that was the end of that B.S. call (in show business, you get a lot of them). And lo and behold, she called me back an hour later and agreed with my price, and said she would need me there for two day. She gave me an address and date to be on set.

I arrived on the set and someone showed me to my trailer. They explained the concept of the video to me and what Pac wanted me to do. I went to see wardrobe and makeup. After that I walked around the set meeting people, when suddenly there is a mini-commotion behind me. I turned around to see Pac and his crew there. He was dressed in slacks, a dress shirt and dress shoes. I was surprised by his stature. He wasn't a big guy. He was about 5'7" and looked like he weighed about 140 pounds. He had big eyes with long eyelashes, and a huge smile. This female photographer began taking a few shots of me and grabbed Pac and said to him, "come over here Pac and take a picture with Pierre." He had the biggest smile on his face when he saw me and started laughing. I was surprised by his enthusiasm with me, because I didn't know him and he had never met me. Pac was like, *"Ah shyt, that's my man right there. You're a funny dude!"* and he gave me a hug. As the photographer went to take the photo, people start jumping into the shot (there went my solo shot with someone who would become a rap legend). They took him away and he said he'd holla at me later.

A few hours later I was in my trailer when a new red Lamborghini pulled up. It was a gift from Suge Knight to Tupac. I thought, *"Damn, Suge's a nice dude. I might have to work for him!* Sadly, after Pac's death I found out a lot of things Pac had or that had been given to him were in Death Row's or Suge's name, so they weren't really his. They say Pac made Death Row $100 million, but after his death his estate was worth only a half million dollars.

I walked around and watched the video being shot, just waiting for my time to perform. I noticed Tupac's attire wasn't thugged out and he was surrounded by many children in the video. This was strange because he always had this thug aura about him. Remember, this was at the height of the East Coast-West Coast beef. I went back to my trailer and chilled for about an hour, when I heard a knock on the door. I yelled, "Come in" and Pac walked in and sat in a chair, looking tired as hell. I later found out he was working like crazy then, recording songs, making movies, and shooting videos back to back, day after day. Because he was out on bail and might have to go back to jail, Suge wanted him to have enough material for the public while he was in jail. I asked him why he picked me to be in his video and he told me that while he was in jail, he would see me on BET's *Comicview* and thought I was funny as hell. We both talked about the time he spent in Baltimore and how I was from the D.C.-Maryland area. I asked him why he was dressed up and not wearing "thug" gear in this video. I will always remember him telling me he was trying to change his image, and that he was tired of this whole East coast/West coast beef. We chopped it up a little more until someone came to get him and he left.

About an hour later, Kadafi (a member of the *Outlawz*) came to my trailer and said Pac wanted to see me in his trailer, so I went. When I got in there, the smoke was thick and the drinks were flowing (damn, this was noon!). As I entered, Pac started laughing and said, "Nigga say something funny." I thought, *"Damn, now I'm the court jester on the set?"* Now you know I can Jone, so I started lighting dudes up in the trailer. We had a good time, and the next thing I knew Pac and I had to go on set. I saw him again the next day as we shot more scenes together. Pac really liked me and invited me to come hang with him at his *Outlawz* hideaway home in the valley a few days later. I went over there, and saw that it was a nice house tucked away on a back street, lined with many low hanging trees. I wondered to myself who they were trying to hide from. Inside it looked like a typical young rapper's house. Shyt all over, sparsely furnished, a few girls, dudes smoking, playing domino's and a few pit bulls running around. Pac wasn't there. I kicked it outside for a minute, and since that wasn't really my scene, I left.

In August 1996, I was performing at the Comedy Store and Kadafi approached me in the hallway and said Pac wanted to talk to me. He was over in the main room. I followed him over to this huge group of guys and in the middle was Pac, laughing at me as usual and asking when I was going on that stage (the club has three different showcase rooms). I told him I was performing in one of the other rooms. He offered me some Cristal, which I declined. I told him I'd see him around and thanked him for putting me in his video.

A few weeks later he was shot and killed in Las Vegas. And sadly, Kadafi would meet the same fate a few weeks later. When I knew Pac, he wasn't yet the icon he later became, so I didn't see him that way. But I will say he had an aura about him that made you feel like he was both a star and your homeboy at the same time. I'm glad I met him.

Tyler Perry *(Actor, Director)*

I had heard about Tyler many times before I met him. People would always ask me, *"Do you know Tyler Perry? He does plays."* And I would say, *"No. Is he funny? Is he a comedian?"*

In January 2003, I was in Memphis rehearsing for a play called *Something She Can Feel* in a hotel where I was staying. I was at the front desk standing in line behind a young lady who was getting information. I noticed a nicely dressed man wearing a long trench coat, leaning against the wall nearby. He was tall and handsome, dressed like a model out of GQ magazine. I could tell he wasn't just an average brother off the streets. She would ask the front desk clerk a question, then look back at him and get an approval look or nod. I knew he was somebody, I just didn't know who. I could tell he had that *Je ne sais qua* before he even opened his mouth. He caught my eye and said to me, "I like your work." I said, "Thanks." The young lady finished her business and went back to him and I proceeded to the front desk clerk. But he struck me as odd. You know how sometimes there's something that just doesn't seem right with someone? Not necessarily in a bad way, but you just can't put your finger on it. Well my first encounter with this man was like that.

The next day we had to get feedback on the play. We had done a rehearsal show in front of a live audience a few days earlier in Pine Bluff, Arkansas, and filmed it. I was such a nervous wreck because I was afraid of messing up; this was my first live play. This ain't the movies. If you mess up you can't yell "cut" and start over. When we finished that show I was drenched with sweat. As far as comedy and timing, I noticed a lot of mistakes we made in the play that night in Arkansas. This day we'd watch the tape and take notes. As I walked in the conference room, who was sitting next to the director and his assistant? The well-dressed guy from the previous day. He was introduced to us as Tyler Perry. The notes he gave us were the exact things I noticed. I thought to myself, this guy knows comedy and timing. I later found out that many of the actors in our play had toured with him for many years, even our director, and that's why they invited him to give notes. He was in town at that time performing with one of his own plays, *Class Reunion*.

Tyler doesn't know it, but he helped me as a stage actor. He invited us to the opening night of his play that night in Memphis. We get to the show and it's was packed. We had seats right in the middle of the tenth row; couldn't ask for better. The lights were still up and the show was just about to start, and people were still trying to get into their seats (you know us Black folks, always late). All of a sudden I heard this voice coming out of the house speakers, and what a voice it was! It was Tyler Perry, doing the voice of Madea. I had never seen or heard Madea before. Madea started to talk about people coming in late, what they were wearing, etc. He had the crowd in stitches before the show even started. Brilliant, if I do say so myself.

This was where Tyler helped me as a stage actor. He played two characters: a bellhop in the first half of the play, and Madea in the second half. During a scene in the second half, an actress called him by his first half character's name (the bellhop). Now everyone in the audience heard it, and Tyler (as Madea) looked at her and then the audience and back to her and said, "You know damn well I'm not that character, I'm Madea, now," and the crowd went wild. At that point I said to myself, don't be afraid if you mess up in live theatre. Roll with it and laugh with the audience. There were many nights where something went wrong, and we and the audience just rolled with it. Hell, it's *live* theatre, things go wrong.

We toured with that play and had some heavy hitting urban play actors on board. I truly got my live theatre feet wet with some true professionals. But with those folks come egos. BIG egos. And after a few months of in-fighting, the play fell apart. That was such a shame because it was good; real good. I've seen many plays after that and ours was one of the best.

Tyler would go on to become a huge star, putting out movies and TV shows. But after seeing Tyler live, I was never afraid of live theatre again. Thank you Tyler, for being there when I needed you without even knowing it.

Wendy Williams *(Radio and Talk show host)*

I was working at the Laff House in Philly in January 1999. I was in the limo heading to do a morning radio show and I had the driver turn to the station I would be on, so I could get a feel of the show. I heard this woman interviewing Left Eye of TLC by phone and she was asking some hard personal questions. I listened as the questions became more invasive, and I could tell Left Eye was getting unnerved. I thought, *"Who is this asshole of a morning jock?"* I asked the driver who she was and he said, "That's Wendy Williams. She got kicked out of New York recently, and now she's here in Philly." I could see why. I knew I would have my hands full, but I've been from the streets of comedy longer than I have been a stand-up comedian, so I was like, *"bring it on!"*

When I got to the station I was led into the booth, and came face-to-face with the one and only, Wendy Williams. I was taken aback by her look. She was a big woman, broad shoulders, a massive weave and a lot of makeup. You know how when you hear somebody first before seeing he or she, and you form a mental image of them? Well I didn't form this one. She didn't look bad, just a bit diva-ish.

When the interview started, she quickly shot some jabs about Halle. She asked me if Halle's breath stank during our kissing scene. Then she asked me about Halle and David Justice, because Halle was going through a divorce at that time. I thought, *"This woman is reaching, and sounds like a bit of a hater."* She tried to take the interview in a downward direction, but she didn't know who she was dealing with. The interview ended within five minutes. I guess she saw it wasn't going down that road. I had an unfavorable view of her when I left the station.

The next time I ran into her was a few years later in the studio in New York City. She had gotten herself back on New York radio in the afternoon, and I was in performing at Caroline's on Broadway. She was kind enough to let me come in for an interview again. She seemed a lot friendlier and asked more reasonable questions. We had a good time and this time when I left, I felt better about her. I think the ups and downs of her radio career started to get to her, and now she probably backed off when needed.

She now has a hugely successful syndicated TV show and I usually catch it when I'm on the treadmill at the gym. When it comes to "Wendy Williams," I get it and I get her. She means no harm, she just wants to entertain. She also talks about herself at times, which I can respect as a comic. When people get all up in arms with her I tell them, don't put so much weight on what she says or does. Chill out a bit and either go along for the ride or change the channel. So, Wendy Williams, "how *you* doin'?"

Wesley Snipes *(Actor)*

Around the summer of 1997, I was performing at the Uptown Comedy Club in the Buckhead section of Atlanta. After the show, I saw Wesley outside. He came up to me and told me how much he enjoyed my show and shook my hand. This dude had a fuckin' Kung Fu grip! When I got my hand back I had to count my fingers AND TOES. What I did notice was the alcohol on his breath, so I chalked up the hard handshake to him maybe being a little tipsy. When he walked away I was excited that he liked my show, but pissed because he damn near broke my hand. Look, I don't give weak handshakes, but let me have a chance to prepare for the *ultimate* handshake. They say he's the reason Halle is a little deaf in one ear. If that's true I can easily see why.

The next time I ran into Wesley was around the time of the Tyson/Lewis fight in Memphis. We were at B.B. King's club the night before the fight, and the club was jammed packed with all the who's who. You name them, if they were Black and famous, they were there. I was sat next to Wesley in VIP, and he went to shake my hand. I thought, *"Not this time brother"* and I grabbed his hand firmly. I know it was only for a second or two, but I felt like we were doing a "hand standoff" for like five minutes. We pulled away with respect for each other and enjoyed the evening.

I'm not much of a drinker. Every blue moon, I'll have a drink. But this nigga right here, this *nigga* right *here*. If it had a proof on it, it was going down. To his credit, he could handle his liquor. He was pretty cool to the fans that came over to our table. We had a great time and I enjoyed the fact that I had a chance to kick it with "Nino Brown."

Will Smith *(Actor)* & Jada Pinkett-Smith *(Actress)*

Jada and Will were under the same management I was in 1996, Handprint Management. One night in July, she and Will decided to catch my act at the Comedy Store. I knew of Jada's work and thought she was an excellent actress; she was also from near my hometown. I always have a soft spot for people who came up around my area because I feel like I understand their struggle to make it out of that area, and the non-supportive system you usually encounter. So I was excited that she was coming with her then-boyfriend, Will Smith.

Now Will and I had met weeks earlier because I was the warm-up guy for *The Fresh Prince of Bel Air*. That's the person that keeps live audiences entertained between sets during TV show tapings. He was pretty much the same in person as you see on TV, always smiling and laughing. I thought he was a bit goofy. Nobody laughs that much. Ain't nobody THAT happy all the damn time. But I guess if you have a show named after you, a hot new movie, *Independence Day,* and a fine girlfriend, I guess yo ass would be smiling and giggling all the damn time too.

I watched how Will handled himself on the set of the *Fresh Prince*. That boy was good. He kept a smile on his face, didn't lose his temper, and interacted with the audience during breaks, damn near doing my job. I was surprised at how big and tall he was; many times artists are so small. At lunch, Will came over and sat with the crew for a minute and chopped it up. I've heard stories about stars wanting nothing to do with cast and crew so I was surprised that he was talking to us.

Will drove a new green S500 Mercedes coupe that I envied. I would watch him leave the parking lot of our management office and imagine I would one day own a $100,000 car. Now I wasn't doing too shabby myself at the time. I had a BMW 528i and a Toyota Landcruiser. But I definitely wasn't in his league. He was making sitcom star money, and I was making warm-up guy for the sitcom star money.

The night they came to see me was great. I rocked the house; I really wanted to do well for them because I wanted them to feel like I was worthy of being with their management team also. When my set was over, they stepped outside and spoke with me while waiting for their car to be brought over from valet. When people saw who I was talking to, they came from everywhere. White people can be corny at times. White guys were congratulating Will on kicking Alien ass and saving the world, and seeming to be thankful. Hello folks, it was a movie, it was *not* real. As that S500 was pulled up by the valet and they got in and drove off, all I could think was, "*One day*."

I would only see Will and Jada a few more times, because the manager that brought me into the company had left, and I wanted to be loyal so I decided to stay with him. Big mistake. One thing I can say about Will and Jada is that they've turned into the perfect Hollywood couple. They, along with their kids would have successful careers, raise a happy family, and keep their heads on straight. Many Hollywood couples should take notes from them.

Xzibit *(Rapper, Actor)*

Around the summer of 1996, I was hanging with Dr. Dre and one of his main producers, Mel Man, and became quick friends with him. Mel LOVED for me to Jone; as soon as I'd see him, he'd start with me, and then try to get me to get on someone else. Mel Man is from Pittsburgh's Hill District. This might be the roughest neighborhood in Pittsburgh that I ever went to. His sister was having a fashion show, and he wanted Xzibit and me to attend. When I got to the airport, I ran into Mel Man and Xzibit, and he greeted me with a big smile. Xzibit loves to laugh and Jone also. It's funny, before that all I knew of him was his famous scowl and hardcore demeanor. This was long before *Pimp My Ride.* Mel Man went all out. First class everything, flight, hotel, limo, you name it. (Damn, Dre must be paying well.)

We were taken to Mel Man's *hood* and people came out from all over. Mel had become a success story around there, and he was bringing his new friends with him. Xzibit handled things cool, very friendly and willing to show love to all, and they were on him. We went to an after party at this club by the water and Mel Man had a few uncles shadowing us. These dudes were in their 40's and 50's, quiet and all wore big coats (street people know what I'm talking about). Hello! It was summertime! OK, OK, that means they were strapped.

While we were in the club, a fight broke out with one of Mel's homeboys and since Mel had the clout, they threw the other dude out. Having dealt with enough street dudes, I know that when something breaks out and you're involved, and they throw the other dude(s) out, it's best you leave right behind them. People will plot while you're still in the club. The club let out and I felt a little eerie and was ready to leave, but everyone had crowded around our limo. Mel told Xzibit and I to take the limo back to the hotel and he'd ride back with his cousin and a few girls, and his Uncles would follow him.

I remember a young aspiring rapper wanted an autograph from X while he was sitting in the limo and he gave him one. Then he wanted a picture and X got out and gave him one. But X's mind was occupied with Mel and wanting to make sure he was straight. This young rapper kept trying to talk to him, and I could see it was getting to X. He went off, and told the dude to get the fuck out of his face, before he beat the dog shit out of his bitch ass. The look on the young dude's face was priceless. But in all honesty, he was being a little pushy.

We got back in the limo and headed back to the hotel. We got there and a few minutes later, Mel came back in a car riddled with bullets. The guy Mel's cousin had gotten in a fight with had followed him and as they stopped at a light, he stepped out his car and fired at their car. But unbeknownst to the shooter, Mel's uncles were behind him in another car and fired back at the dude, who escaped by the hair on his chin.

What a way to first meet "X to the Z." We sat up that night talking about all the things he wanted to do in show business. I found him to be engaging and very smart. And by the looks of his career, he did exactly what he said he wanted to do. And he's also not a bad actor.

Outro

I'm glad you decided to take this retrospective journey with me. As I wrote this book, it gave me a chance to realize how blessed I have been. Very few people can say they are doing exactly what they have dreamed of doing and making a living at it. To know that I was able to pick a career and stick with it. I'm very grateful for the opportunity to live out my dreams.

I think everyone in this book should be commended for reaching the heights they have in their respective careers. The simple fact that I could write about these people and that you're interested enough to want to read about them is an accomplishment in itself.

I have had the opportunity to meet some very talented and special people. People that others only dream about meeting. I feel honored to have had the opportunities to spend some private times with these people. I also paid a heavy price for these opportunities. I can't lie. There have been times I wished I had taken the road more traveled, gone to college and gotten a steady job, but that thought always seems to quickly dissipate.

I will continue on my journey in this business until my last breath because this is me. I love you, the fans, so much. I feel like I owe you this. So, if you see your boy in the streets, holla! You know I'll show you the same love you show me.

After all I've been through, this is me today. Still smiling.